GOD'S DESIGN
FOR CHEMISTRY

D1290733

PROPERTIES
OF MATTER

Debbie Lawrence and Richard Lawrence

God's Design for Chemistry is a complete chemistry curriculum for elementary aged children. The books in this series are designed for use in the Christian homeschool, and provide easy to use lessons that will encourage children to see God's hand in everything around them.

2nd Printing: March 2006

Copyright © 2004 by Debbie Lawrence and its licensors.
All Rights Reserved

ISBN: 1-893345-79-3

Cover design: Brandie Lucas
Layout: Diane King
Editor: Gary Vaterlaus

No part of this book may be reproduced in any form or by any means without written permission from the author and publisher other than: (1) the specific pages within the book that are designed for single family/classroom use, and (2) as brief quotations quoted in a review.

All scripture quotations are taken from the New King James Version®. Copyright © 1982 by Thomas Nelson, Inc. Used by permission. All rights reserved.

The publisher and authors have made every reasonable effort to ensure that the activities recommended in this book are safe when performed as instructed but assume no responsibility for any damage caused or sustained while conducting the experiments and activities in this book. It is the parents', guardians', and/or teachers' responsibility to supervise all recommended activities.

Published by *Answers in Genesis*, PO Box 510, Hebron, Kentucky 42080

Printed in the United States of America

You may contact the authors at: info@rdeducation.com; (970) 686-5744

www.AnswersInGenesis.org

CONTENTS

WELCOME TO
GOD'S DESIGN FOR CHEMISTRY

God's Design for Chemistry is a series that has been designed for use in teaching chemistry to children in grades 3-7. It is divided into two books: *Properties of Matter* and *Properties of Atoms and Molecules*. Each book has approximately 35 lessons as well as a unit project that ties all of the lessons together.

In addition to the lessons, special features in each book include biographical information on interesting people as well as interesting facts pages to make the subject more fun and a little less dusty.

Please use the books in this series as a guide and feel free to add to each lesson. Although this is a complete curriculum, the information included here is just a beginning. A resource guide is included in Appendix B to help you find additional information and resources. Also, a supply list of items needed is included at the beginning of each lesson. A master list of all supplies needed for the entire book can be found in Appendix C.

If you wish to cover the material in this series in one year you should plan on covering approximately 2 lessons per week. The time required for each lesson varies depending on how much additional information you want to include, but you can plan on about 45 minutes per lesson. Older children can do quizzes, tests or additional activities on non-lesson days if you choose to do science every day.

If you wish to cover material in more depth, you may add additional information and take a longer period of time to cover all the material.

WHY TEACH CHEMISTRY?

Maybe you hate science or you just hate teaching it. Maybe you love science but don't quite know how to teach it to your children. Maybe science just doesn't seem as important as some of those other subjects you need to teach. Maybe you need a little motivation. If any of these descriptions fits you, then please consider the following.

It is not uncommon to question the need to teach your kids hands-on science in elementary school. We could argue that the knowledge gained in science will be needed later in life in order for your children to be more productive and well-rounded adults. We could argue that teaching your children science also teaches them logical and inductive thinking and reasoning skills, which are tools they will need to be more successful. We could argue that science is a necessity in this technological world in which we live. While all of these arguments are true, none of them are the main reason that we should teach our children science. The most important reason to teach science in elementary school is to give your children an understanding that God is our Creator, and the Bible can be trusted. Teaching science from a creation perspective is one of the best ways to reinforce your children's faith in God and to help them counter the evolutionary propaganda they face every day.

God is the Master Creator of everything. His handiwork is all around us. Our Great Creator put in place all of the laws of physics, biology and chemistry. These laws were put here for us to see His wisdom and power. In science, we see the hand of God at work more than in any other subject. Romans 1:20 says, "For since the creation of the world His invisible attributes are clearly seen, being understood by the things that are made, even His eternal power and Godhead, so that they [men] are without excuse" (NKJV). We need to help our children see God as Creator of the world around them so they will be able to recognize God and follow Him.

The study of chemistry helps us understand and appreciate the amazing way everything God created works together. The study of atoms and molecules and how different substances react with each other reveals an amazing design, even at the smallest level of life. Understanding the carbon, nitrogen and water cycles helps our children see that God has a plan to keep everything working together.

It's fun to teach chemistry! It's interesting too. The elements of chemistry are all around us. Children naturally like to combine things to see what will happen. You just need to direct their curiosity.

Finally, teaching chemistry is easy. You won't have to try to find strange materials for experiments or do dangerous things to learn about chemistry. Chemistry is as close as your kitchen or your own body.

How Do I Teach Science?

In order to teach any subject you need to understand how people learn. People learn in different ways. Most people, and children in particular, have a dominant or preferred learning style in which they absorb and retain information more easily.

If your child's dominant style is:

Auditory – he needs to not only hear the information but he needs to hear himself say it. This child needs oral presentation as well as oral drill and repetition.

Visual – he needs things he can see. This child responds well to flashcards, pictures, charts, models, etc.

Kinesthetic – he needs active participation. This child remembers best through games, hands-on activities, experiments and field trips.

Also, some people are more relational while others are more analytical. Your relational child needs to know who the people are, why this is important and how it will affect him personally. Your analytical child, however, wants just the facts.

If you are trying to teach more than one child, you will probably have to deal with more than one learning style. Therefore, you need to present your lessons in several different ways so that each child can grasp and retain the information. You need to give them a reason to learn it.

To help you with this, we have divided each lesson into three sections. The first section introduces the topic. It is the "just the facts" part of the lesson for the analytical child. This section is marked by the icon. The second section is the observation and hands-on section denoted by the 🔍 icon. This section helps your visual and kinesthetic learners. The final section is the summary and review section denoted by the 🎁 icon, representing wrapping up the lesson. This oral review helps your auditory learners. Also included in this section is the applications part of the lesson to help your relational child appreciate what he has learned. We have included periodic biographies to help your child appreciate the great men and women who have gone before us in the field of science.

We suggest a threefold approach to each lesson:

📢 INTRODUCE THE TOPIC

- We give a brief description of the facts. Frequently you will want to add more information than the bare essentials given in this book. This section of each lesson is written as if we were talking to your child. In addition to reading this section aloud, you may wish to do one or more of the following:

- Read a related book with your child.

- Write things on the board to help your visual child.

- Give some history of the subject. We provide some historical sketches to help you, but you may want to add more.

- Ask questions to get your child thinking about the subject.

🔍 MAKE OBSERVATIONS AND DO EXPERIMENTS

- One or more hands-on projects are suggested for each lesson. This section of each lesson is written to the parent/teacher.

- Have your child observe the topic for him/herself whenever possible.

🎁 WRAP IT UP

- The "What did we learn?" section has review questions.

- The "Taking it further" section encourages your child to

o Draw conclusions

o Make applications of what was learned

o Add extended information to what was covered in the lesson

- The "FUN FACT" section adds fun information.
(Questions with answers are provided to help you wrap up the lesson.)

By teaching all three parts of the lesson, you will be presenting the material in a way that all learning styles can both relate to and remember.

Also, this method relates directly to the scientific method and will help your child think more scientifically. Don't panic! The "scientific method" is just a way to logically examine a subject and learn from it. Briefly, the steps of the scientific method are:

1. Learn about a topic.

2. Ask a question.

3. Make a hypothesis (a good guess).

4. Design an experiment to test your hypothesis.

5. Observe the experiment and collect data.

6. Draw conclusions. (Does the data support your hypothesis?)

Note: It's okay to have a "wrong hypothesis." That's how we learn. Be sure to try to understand why you got a different result than you expected.

Our lessons will help your child begin to approach problems in a logical, scientific way.

HOW DO I TEACH CREATION VS. EVOLUTION?

We are constantly bombarded by evolutionary ideas about life, which prompt many questions. Is a living being just a collection of chemicals? Did life begin as a random combination of chemicals? Can life be recreated in a laboratory? What does the chemical evidence tell us about the earth? The Bible answers these questions and this book accepts the historical accuracy of the Bible as written. We believe this is the only way we can teach our children to trust that everything God says is true.

There are 5 common views of the origins of life and the age of the earth:

1. Historical biblical account – Each day of creation in Genesis is a normal day of about 24 hours in length, in which God created everything that exists. The earth is only thousands of years old, as determined by the genealogies in the Bible.

2. Progressive creation - The idea that God created various creatures to replace other creatures that died out over millions of years. Each of the days in Genesis represents a long period of time (day-age theory) and the earth is billions of years old.

3. Gap theory – The idea that there was a long, long time between what happened in Genesis 1:1 and what happened in Genesis 1:2. During this time, the "fossil record" was supposed

to have formed, and millions of years of Earth history supposedly passed.

4. Theistic evolution – The idea that God used the process of evolution over millions of years (involving struggle and death) to bring about what we see today.

5. Naturalistic evolution – The view that there is no God and evolution of all life forms happened by purely naturalistic processes over billions of years.

Any theory that tries to add the evolutionary timeframe with creation presupposes that death entered the world before Adam sinned, which contradicts what God has said in His Word. The view that the Earth (and its "fossil record") is hundreds of millions of years old damages the Gospel message. God's completed creation was "very good" at the end of the sixth day (Genesis 1:31). Death entered this perfect paradise *after* Adam disobeyed God's command. It was the punishment for Adam's sin (Genesis 2:16-17; 3:19; Romans 5:12-19).

The first animal death occurred when God killed at least one animal, shedding its blood, to make clothes for Adam and Eve (Genesis 3:21). If the Earth's "fossil record" (filled with death, disease and thorns) formed over millions of years before Adam appeared (and before he sinned), then death no longer would be the penalty for sin. Death, the "last enemy" (1 Corinthians 15:26), and diseases (such as cancer) would instead be part of the original creation that God labeled "very good." No, it is clear that the "fossil record" formed some time *after* Adam sinned—not many millions of years before. Most fossils were formed as a result of the worldwide Genesis Flood.

When viewed from a biblical perspective, the scientific evidence clearly supports a recent creation by God, and not naturalistic evolution and millions of years. The volume of evidence supporting the biblical creation account is substantial and cannot be adequately covered in this book. If you would like more information on this topic, please see the resource guide in Appendix B. To help get you started, just a few examples of evidence supporting a recent creation are given below:

• **Evolutionary Myth:** Life evolved from non-life when chemicals randomly combined together to produce amino acids and then proteins that then produced living cells. **The Truth:** The chemical requirements for DNA and proteins to line up just right to create life could not have happened through purely natural processes. The process of converting DNA information into proteins requires at least 75 different protein molecules. But each and every one of these 75 proteins must be synthesized in the first place by the process in which they themselves are involved. How could the process begin without the presence of all the necessary proteins? Could all 75 proteins have arisen by chance in just the right place at just the right time?[1] Dr. Gary Parker says this is like the chicken and the egg problem. The obvious conclusion is that both the DNA and proteins must have been functional from the beginning, otherwise life could not exist. The best explanation for the existence of these proteins and DNA is that God created them.[2]

• **Evolutionary Myth:** Stanley Miller created life in a test tube, thus demonstrating that the early earth had the conditions necessary for life to begin. **The Truth:** Although Miller was able to create amino acids from raw chemicals in his famous experiment, he did not create anything

---

[1] John P. Marcus, in: Ashton, J., ed., *In Six Days: Why 50 scientists choose to believe in creation*, Master Books, 2000, 177.

[2] Gary Parker, *Creation Facts of Life*, Creation Life Publishers, 1994, 24-28.

close to life or even the ingredients of life. There are four main problems with Miller's experiment. First, he left out oxygen because he knew that oxygen corrodes and destroys amino acids very quickly. However, rocks found in every layer of the earth indicate that oxygen has always been a part of the earth's atmosphere. Second, Miller included ammonia gas and methane gas. Ammonia gas would not have been present in any large quantities because it would have been dissolved in the oceans. And there is no indication in any of the rock layers that methane has ever been a part of the earth's atmosphere. Third, Miller used a spark of electricity to cause the amino acids to form, simulating lightning. However, this spark more quickly destroyed the amino acids than built them up, so to keep the amino acids from being destroyed, Miller used specially designed equipment to siphon off the amino acids before they could be destroyed. This is not what would have happened in nature. And finally, although Miller did produce amino acids, they were not the kinds of amino acids that are needed for life as we know it. Most of the acids were ones that actually break down proteins, not build them up.[3]

• **Evolutionary Myth:** Living creatures are just a collection of chemicals. **The Truth:** It is true that cells are made of specific chemicals. However, a dead animal is made of the same chemicals as it was when it was living, but it cannot become alive again. What makes the chemicals into a living creature is the result of the organization of the substances, not just the substances themselves. Dr. Parker again uses an example. An airplane is made up of millions of non-flying parts; however, it can fly because of the design and organization of those parts. Similarly, plants and animals are alive because God created the chemicals in a specific way for them to be able to live.[4] A collection of all the right parts is not life.

• **Evolutionary Myth:** Chemical evidence points to an earth that is billions of years old. **The Truth:** Much of the chemical evidence actually points to a young earth. For example, radioactive decay in the earth's crust produces helium atoms that rise to the surface and enter the atmosphere. Assuming that the rate of helium production has always been constant (an evolutionary assumption), the maximum age for the atmosphere could only be 2 million years. This is much younger than the 4+ billion years claimed by evolutionists. And there are many ideas that could explain the presence of helium that would indicate a much younger age than 2 million years.[5] Similarly, salt accumulates in the ocean over time. Evolutionists claim that life evolved in a salty ocean 3-4 billion years ago. If this were true and the salt has continued to accumulate over billions of years, the ocean would be too salty for anything to live in by now. Using the most conservative possible values (those that would give the oldest possible age for the oceans), scientists have calculated that the ocean must be less than 62 million years. That number is based on the assumption that nothing has affected the rate at which the salt is accumulating. However, the Genesis Flood would have drastically altered the amount of salt in the ocean, dissolving much sodium from land rocks.[6] Thus, the chemical evidence does not support an earth that is billions of years old.

---

[3] Ken Ham, et al., *War of the Worldviews*, Master Books, 2006, 15-24. See also www.AnswersInGenesis.org/origin.

[4] Parker, op. cit., 29-30.

[5] See Dr. Don DeYoung, *Thousands…not billions*, Master Books, 2005. See also: www.AnswersInGenesis.org/helium.

[6] John D. Morris, Ph.D., *The Young Earth*, Creation Life Publishers 1994, 83-87. See also www.AnswersInGenesis.org/creation/v21/i1/seas.asp

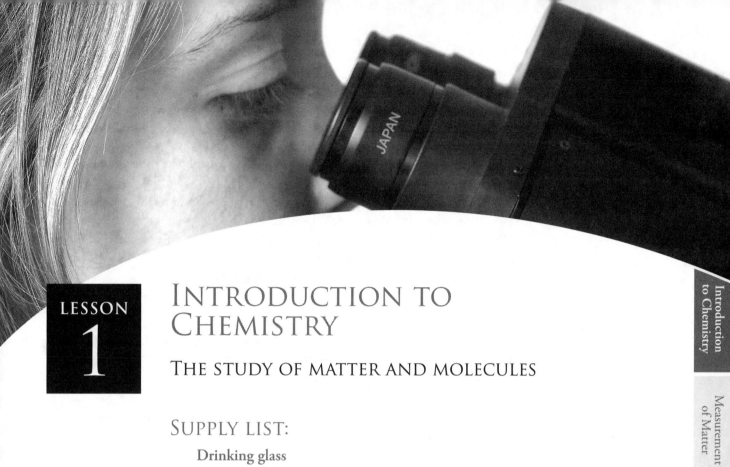

LESSON 1

INTRODUCTION TO CHEMISTRY

THE STUDY OF MATTER AND MOLECULES

SUPPLY LIST:

Drinking glass
Baking soda
Vinegar

Chemistry may sound like a big word and a difficult subject to study, but it's not. Chemistry is simply the study of matter and matter is anything that has mass and takes up space. Some examples of matter are water, wood, air, food, paper, your pet skunk or your little brother. So if you are interested in learning more about anything around you, then you are ready to learn about chemistry.

Chemists are scientists who study what things are made of, how they react to each other and how they react to their environment. Chemistry is the study of the basic building blocks of life and the world.

In chemistry you will learn about atoms and molecules. You will learn about how substances combine to make other substances. You will find out how a substance changes form and you will discover that God created our world with such intricate designs that we may never fully understand how everything works.

God has established laws that govern how chemicals react and how matter changes. Many of these laws seem mysterious because they happen on an atomic level. Although, these changes cannot be seen with the naked eye, the results of these laws can be seen all around us. As you study atoms and molecules you will begin to understand these laws and appreciate the beauty of God's design on the tiny level of the atom.

GOD'S DESIGN FOR CHEMISTRY
PROPERTIES OF MATTER

Introduction
to Chemistry

Measurement
of Matter

States of Matter

Classifications
of Matter

Solutions

Food Chemistry

Unit Activity
& Conclusion

CHEMISTRY IS FUN:

As you will learn in the upcoming lessons, some materials are very stable and do not change easily. Other materials are very reactive and easily combine with other substances to make a new substance. For a fun experiment try the following:

Place 1 teaspoon of baking soda in a drinking cup. Pour 1 tablespoon of vinegar into the cup. Now watch the reaction!

Vinegar is an acid and baking soda is a base. Acids and bases easily combine together to form salts. In this reaction they also produce a gas. Can you guess what that gas might be? It is carbon dioxide.

WHAT DID WE LEARN?

What is matter? (Anything that has mass and takes up space?)

Does air have mass? (Yes. It may seem like there is nothing there, but even though air is very light, it still has mass. The air contains molecules that take up space.)

What do chemists study? (The way matter reacts with other matter and the environment.)

TAKING IT FURTHER

Would you expect to see the same reaction each time you combine baking soda and vinegar? (Yes, because God designed certain laws for matter to follow so we would expect it to react the same way each time.)

Introduction to Chemistry

Measurement of Matter

States of Matter

Classifications of Matter

Solutions

Food Chemistry

Unit Activity & Conclusion

LESSON 2

THE SCIENTIFIC METHOD

HOW DO SCIENTISTS DO IT?

SUPPLY LIST:

3 empty soda pop or other bottles	Masking tape
Yeast	Marker
Cloth tape measure or string	Sugar
Molasses	3 identical balloons
Thermometer	Measuring cup and spoons

1 copy of "Scientific Method Worksheet" per child (pg. 7)

What is a scientist? A scientist is someone who uses observations and a systematic method to study the physical world and how everything in it works. Scientists can only study things that can be observed, measured and tested. Scientists cannot study history, philosophy or religion because these things cannot be tested and observed.

We must understand that there are two major types of science: *operational* science and *origins* science. Operational science involves discovering how things operate in today's Creation—repeatable and observable events in the present. This is science as we normally think of it. Origins science, however, deals with the origin of things in the past—unique, unrepeatable, unobservable events. There is an essential difference between how the two work. Operational science involves experimentation in the here and now. Origins science deals with how something came into existence in the past and so cannot be observed, tested or repeated.

How the world came to be is a matter of origins science. We cannot repeat the creation of the world, or travel back in time to see how it happened. But, we do have an eyewitness who told us how it happened—God, in His Word has revealed to us that He made everything in six days.

Over the centuries, scientists have developed a way of approaching problems that is called the scientific method. This is not a set of rules, but

3

Introduction
to Chemistry

Measurement
of Matter

States of Matter

Classifications
of Matter

Solutions

Food Chemistry

Unit Activity
& Conclusion

a way of thinking. It is a logical, systematic approach to solving problems. In general, the scientific method has five steps.

1. Learn about something – make observations

2. Ask a question – identify a problem

3. Propose a solution – make an hypothesis (a good guess)

4. Design a way to test your hypothesis– test your idea, record observations and results

5. Check if your results support your hypothesis – make a conclusion.

Different books will list different steps or ways to perform the scientific method, but the ideas will still be the same.

You probably use this method to solve simple problems every day without even realizing it. For example, if you own a houseplant you probably learned that plants need sunshine and water to grow. You identify a problem when you notice that your plant looks droopy. You make a hypothesis and guess that the plant needs to be watered. You test your hypothesis by watering the plant. Then you check to see if your hypothesis was right by seeing if the plant looks better after you watered it. If it does, you conclude that your hypothesis was right. This is a very simple example of how you use the scientific method frequently.

Now let's look at each step of the scientific process in a little more detail. First, you need to learn about a topic. This can be done by direct observation using your five senses. You can also do research by reading books or reports. We can and should learn from those who have gone before us. There is no sense in "reinventing the wheel" when we can find out a great deal from others' work.

Second, we can identify a problem by asking a question. This requires curiosity. Ask, "How does this work, why did this happen or what if we tried this?" Almost all great inventions have come about because the inventor asked, "How can we do this a better way?" God gave humans a great amount of curiosity and He wants us to use it to improve our lives and to glorify Him.

Once we identify a problem that needs to be solved or have a question we want to answer, we need to make a guess as to what the answer will be. This answer should be based on what we have observed and learned. For example, if you have a plant that is not growing well, you may ask how you can make it grow better. You have learned that plants not only need water and sunshine, but they also need nutrients. So you guess that your plant is doing poorly because the soil does not have enough nutrients in it. This is a reasonable guess based on what you have learned. It would not be a reasonable guess to say that the plant needs bubble gum to grow better.

The next step is to design a test that will help you decide if your guess is correct. This test or experiment should be set up to only test one thing at a time. If you change two or more things at once you will not know which change gave the observed results. If you move the plant from a dark room

GOD'S DESIGN FOR CHEMISTRY
PROPERTIES OF MATTER

Introduction to Chemistry

Measurement of Matter

States of Matter

Classifications of Matter

Solutions

Food Chemistry

Unit Activity & Conclusion

into a sunny room and feed it more plant food, and then the plant starts growing better, you will not know if the added sunlight or the plant food or a combination of both caused the change. You need to change only one thing at a time. This is called controlling variables. So first, keep the plant in its current location and give it fertilizer. If that helps, you know it needed nutrients. If the plant does not improve, try moving it to a sunny location. Changing only one thing at a time will help you determine the cause of the change.

Finally, after you complete your test, you need to check and see if the results show that your hypothesis is correct or not. It is okay to have a wrong hypothesis! When Thomas Edison was trying to find a material that would work for the light bulb, he tried hundreds of different materials before he found one that worked. The important thing is to try to understand why your hypothesis was wrong, and to try to come up with a better idea to try next time. This is how scientists learn. Also, it is important to share your results so that others do not make the same mistakes you did and so they can learn from your successes as well.

There are limitations to the scientific method. We cannot answer all questions nor can we solve all problems by experimentation. The scientific method can only be used on physical materials. So we cannot use science to establish truth, to make moral judgments or to determine what is right and wrong. We must use God's Word to help us decide these kinds of issues.

Also, the conclusions drawn from experiments can be affected by the scientist's beliefs. For example, many scientists do not believe there is any power outside of the physical world. Therefore, they interpret the results of their tests in light of that idea. When they look at the world today, they think that it got the way it is by natural forces only. However, when a scientist who believes the Bible sees the world, he understands that God created the universe, and that our world has been affected by the curse God put on the earth when Adam disobeyed and by the Great Flood when God judged man's wickedness. Our beliefs affect how we interpret our test results. As Christians, we need to take God's Word first, and then interpret our world in light of what He says, because we know that God cannot lie.

USING THE SCIENTIFIC METHOD:

Let's apply the scientific method to a fun problem:

1. **Learn**: Have you ever watched bread dough rising? The dough starts out as a relatively small lump, but in a few minutes it is tall and fluffy. Bread dough rises because tiny fungi called yeast combine with the sweetener in the dough and give off a gas that lifts up the dough.

2. **Ask a question**: What is the best sweetener to use to make the fluffiest bread?

3. **Make a hypothesis**: Sugar and Molasses are common sweeteners. You guess which one you think would work best. Write your guess on your "Scientific Method Worksheet."

GOD'S DESIGN FOR CHEMISTRY
PROPERTIES OF MATTER

Introduction to Chemistry

Measurement of Matter

States of Matter

Classifications of Matter

Solutions

Food Chemistry

Unit Activity & Conclusion

4. **Design and perform a test**: Remember, you must control your variables. In order to do this we need three identical empty bottles. Put a piece of masking tape on each bottle then number them 1, 2 and 3. In each bottle pour 1 cup of water that is 100°F. Add 1 teaspoon of yeast to each bottle. Do not add anything else to bottle 1. Add 2 tablespoons of sugar to bottle 2 and add 2 tablespoons of molasses to bottle 3. Gently mix the contents of each bottle by swirling the contents for 30 seconds. After mixing, place a balloon over the top of each bottle to catch any gas produced.

After 15 minutes, use a cloth tape measure or string and ruler to measure the circumference of each balloon. Record your measurements on your worksheet. Repeat these measurements every 15 minutes for one hour, recording your results each time.

5. **Check your results**: Did the bottle with your chosen sweetener produce the most gas? Which sweetener would you use to make bread? Answer the questions on your worksheet.

Even if you chose the sweetener that did not produce the most gas, you learned from your experiment. Share your results with someone who did not do the experiment with you, and look for ways to apply the scientific method to other problems.

WHAT DID WE LEARN?

What is the overall job of a scientist? (To systematically study the physical world.)

What are some areas that cannot be studied by science? (Morality, religion, philosophy, history)

What are the five steps of the scientific method? (Learn or observe, ask a question, make a hypothesis, design and perform a test, check the results and draw conclusions.)

TAKING IT FURTHER

Is the theory of evolution operational science or origins science? Why? (Origins science, because it deals with the past and cannot be observed, repeated or tested.)

Why was it necessary to have bottle number 1 in the experiment? (Bottle 1 had only water and yeast. This is called a control. It shows how much gas was produced without a sweetener, so you can tell exactly how much gas was caused by adding the sugar and molasses in the other bottles.)

What other sweeteners could you try in your experiment? (Honey, corn syrup, fruit juice)

What sweeteners were used in the bread at your house? (Look at the ingredients list on the package if you do not bake your own bread.)

Why do you think the company used that sweetener? (Reasons vary, but amount of gas produced, cost, color and taste are all important factors in why companies use the ingredients they do.)

Scientific Method Worksheet

Hypothesis: Do you think sugar or molasses will produce the most gas? _____

Circumference of Balloon

Time	Bottle 1 (no sweetener)	Bottle 2 (sugar)	Bottle 3 (molasses)

Which balloon had the most gas after 1 hour? _____

Did this support your hypothesis? _____

Which sweetener would you use to make your bread? _____

Why might someone choose to use a sweetener that does not produce the most gas?

_____

(Taste, color and texture are all affected by the sweetener used, so even if molasses produces the most gas, you may not like to way it makes your bread taste or look.)

Be sure to show your results to someone who did not do the experiment so they can learn from your results.

Introduction to Chemistry

Measurement of Matter

States of Matter

Classifications of Matter

Solutions

Food Chemistry

Unit Activity & Conclusion

TOOLS OF SCIENCE

USING THE RIGHT TOOL FOR THE JOB

LESSON 3

SUPPLY LIST:

Thermometer
Liquid measuring cup
Metric ruler or meter stick
Digital stop watch
2 cups
1 copy of "Scientific Tools Worksheet" for each child (page 11)

Masking tape
Marker
Small box
Tennis ball

Every person who performs a job requires special tools. A cook needs measuring cups, a mixer, an oven, and pots and pans. A carpenter needs hammers, saws, sanders and many other tools. An athlete needs weight equipment, running shoes, special clothes, ice skates, etc. So also, a scientist needs special tools to do his/her job.

A scientist's main job is to make observations. There are two kinds of observations that a scientist makes: qualitative measurements and quantitative measurements. Qualitative measurements are ones that do not involve numbers. For example, a scientist may observe the color or texture of a material before, during and after an experiment. The main tools that a scientist uses for qualitative measurements are his/her five senses. What qualities might you observe with your five senses? You might see color, bubbles, smoke, size, etc. You could smell odors, hear popping or taste flavors. And you could feel the texture and temperature of the object. Please note that you should **never** taste any unknown substance!

Qualitative measurements are very useful; however, they are dependent on the observer. What one person considers red, another may describe as purple or pink. One person may describe a light as very bright, while another does not. Therefore, qualitative measurements are limited in their usefulness. Whenever possible, scientists choose to make quantitative mea-

surements. Quantitative measurements are observations that involve numerical data.

Scientists have a number of tools to help them make quantitative measurements. These include a balance for measuring mass, graduated cylinders for measuring liquid volumes, thermometers for measuring temperature and spectrometers for measuring the wavelength of light. The list goes on and on. These tools provide unbiased data with which scientists can determine the exact results of an experiment. Quantitative data allows scientists to compare their results with others' results.

Scientists often generate so many numbers in their experiments that it may be difficult to analyze them all, so one of the most important tools a scientist uses is the computer. Computers are ideal for compiling and analyzing large groups of numbers.

Although quantitative data is preferred, it has its limitations as well. Measurement tools have limits on their accuracy. For example, an analog wristwatch with a second hand cannot measure any time period more accurately than to the nearest second. A more accurate digital timer would be needed to measure a reaction that happens in microseconds. A scientist must know the limits of his/her tools and use the best tool for the job. As a scientist, you must learn to make good quantitative measurements and good qualitative observations as well.

LEARNING TO USE YOUR TOOLS:

Complete each task on the "Scientific Tools Worksheet,"

Answers to "Summary" questions on worksheet: Quantitative measurements are more accurate. In general, quantitative measurements are more useful; however, this depends on what you are trying to accomplish. It is not always necessary to make quantitative measurements. You may only need to know if something is warm or melted without having to measure its temperature, for example.

WHAT DID WE LEARN?

What is the main thing a scientist does as he/she studies the physical world? (Make observations.)

What are the two types of measurements that a scientist can make? (Qualitative observations are ones made by the 5 senses without numerical data. Quantitative measurements are made using instruments that generate numerical or other objective data.)

What is the main problem with qualitative measurements? (The observations may vary from person to person because we each perceive things differently.)

GOD'S DESIGN FOR CHEMISTRY
PROPERTIES OF MATTER

Introduction to Chemistry

Measurement of Matter

States of Matter

Classifications of Matter

Solutions

Food Chemistry

Unit Activity & Conclusion

What are some scientific tools used for quantitative measurements? (Balance, graduated cylinder, thermometer, meter stick, spectrometer, etc.)

TAKING IT FURTHER

What qualitative measurements might you make when observing the mixing of vinegar and baking soda? (You might observe that bubbles are produced, that a burning candle placed in the gas produced by the reaction goes out or that the vinegar gives the experiment a strong smell.)

What quantitative measurements might you make when testing the results of mixing vinegar and baking soda? (You might measure the temperature of the vinegar before and after the reaction to see if it changed. You might use litmus paper to test the pH of each substance to see how acidic or basic each substance is, before and after the experiment. There are also more expensive pieces of equipment that can used to test the composition of the gas produced.)

FUN FACT

Qualitative measurements can sometimes be unreliable. Our eyes are easily deceived.

In each picture below, tell whether you think line A or line B is longer.

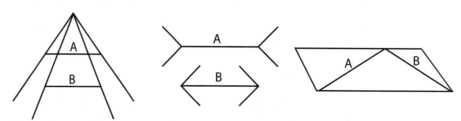

It appears that line A is longer in each picture; however, lines A and B are actually the same length in each picture. Measure each line with a ruler to convince yourself. Quantitative measurements can help prevent mistakes that we might otherwise make.

Introduction to Chemistry

Measurement of Matter

States of Matter

Classifications of Matter

Solutions

Food Chemistry

Unit Activity & Conclusion

Scientific Tools Worksheet

TEST 1: Use masking tape and a marker to label two cups as Cup 1 and Cup 2. Fill Cup 1 with hot tap water and Cup 2 with cold tap water.

    Qualitative measurements: Use your five senses to describe the water in each cup.

Cup 1: _____

Cup 2: _____

    Quantitative measurements: Use a thermometer to measure the temperature of the water in each cup.

The temperature is:

Cup 1: _____   Cup 2: _____

TEST 2: Determine which cup has more water in it.

    Qualitative measurement: Which cup appears to have more water in it? _____

    Quantitative measurement: Pour the contents of Cup 1 into a liquid measuring cup and record the amount of water below. Empty the measuring cup and repeat for Cup 2.

Amount of water in Cup 1 _____   Amount of water in Cup 2 _____

Which cup had the most water in it? _____   How much more water did it have? _____

TEST 3: Observe a small box.

    Qualitative measurement: Describe the size, shape, texture and color of the box.

_____

    Quantitative measurement: Use a ruler or meter stick to measure the box.

Length: _____   Height: _____   Width: _____

TEST 4: Hold a tennis ball at waist height and drop it. Next hold the tennis ball as high as you can reach and drop it. From which height did the ball reach the ground the fastest?

    Qualitative measurement: Describe how long the ball fell each time.

From waist high _____   From high up _____

    Quantitative measurement: Repeat the experiment using a digital stop watch to measure the length of time it takes for the ball to reach the ground after it is realeased.

From waist high _____   From high up _____

Summary

Which type of measurements gave you a more accurate answer? _____

Which type of measurements do you think are more useful? _____

Is it always necessary to make quantitative measurements? _____

LORD KELVIN

(1824-1907)

William Thomson, or Lord Kelvin, was born the fourth child out of seven on June 26, 1824, in Belfast, Ireland. His mother died when he was six years old. His father wrote textbooks and taught math at the University in Belfast and he took on the task of teaching the newest math to William. William had a very close relationship with his father. Over the next several years he learned much about math and wrote several papers. By the time he was 15, he had won a gold medal for his exceptional mathematical ability.

When William Thomson was 16 he entered Cambridge, and 4 years later earned a B.A. degree with high honors. At 22 years of age William was unanimously elected the "Chair of Natural Philosophy" (Physics) at the University of Glasgow, where he stayed until he was 75 years old. Much of William's work involved a theory that electricity and magnetism are related and that electromagnetism and light are related. His work enabled James Clerk Maxwell to form his famous equations describing electromagnetism, which is considered by some to be the most significant achievement of the 19th century. (See Special Feature on Maxwell on page 34.)

Thomson was also very involved in the work behind laying the first transatlantic telegraph cable. After much work and controversy, his design was selected and was successful. Because of the patents he held on some of the equipment used to transmit and receive the signal, he was knighted in 1866, by Queen Victoria and thus became Lord William Thomson of Kelvin, or Lord Kelvin.

Because of the success of the transatlantic cable, Lord Kelvin became a partner in two engineering consulting firms. These firms played a major role in the construction of submarine cables. This made him a wealthy man. With some of that wealth he bought a 126-ton yacht and a large estate.

Lord Kelvin's interest in science was very broad; he did research in electricity, magnetism, thermodynamics, hydrodynamics, geophysics, tides, the shape of the earth, atmospheric electricity, thermal studies of the ground, the earth's rotation and geomagnetism.

In 1884, Lord Kelvin developed an analog computer for measuring and determining the tides in a harbor for any hour, past or future. And he started a company to manufacture these devices. He also went on to publish a textbook on Natural Philosophy or Physics, as it would be called today. He received honorary degrees from all over the world. He was said to be entitled to more letters after his name than any other man in the UK.

Out of all the scientific discoveries made Lord by Kelvin, he is most remembered for his work in accurately measuring temperatures. He developed the temperature scale used by almost all scientists around the world. It is named after him, and is called the Kelvin scale. The Kelvin scale starts at absolute zero, the temperature at which all movement of molecules ceases. This means that zero degrees Kelvin is the coldest anything can get; it's the lowest temperature possible.

In spite of all his great discoveries, Lord Kelvin still made mistakes. In 1900, at an assembly of physicists he stated, "There is nothing new to be discovered in physics now. All that remains is more and more precise measurement." He also stated that heavier-than-air flying machines were impossible. This just goes to show that even a highly respected physicist can make mistakes in his field, even though most of his work has been shown to be correct.

Lord Kelvin was also a very insightful man. In his time many new theories were being developed. Some had merit and others did not. In 1847, he heard about Joule's theory on heat and the motion of heat, which went against the accepted knowledge of the day. Kelvin studied this new theory and later gave his cautious endorsement of it. He also worked to advance the theories of Faraday, Fourier and Joule.

However, when Charles Darwin's theory of evolution was first published, Lord Kelvin opposed it. He believed that all science must be subjected to the same rigors, and he applied what he knew about science to the theory of evolution. Darwin's theory was based on the assumption that life had evolved over a very long time (at that time Darwin believed the earth was millions of years old) during which the forces of nature remained fairly constant, and that nature operated millions of years ago just as it does today. Lord Kelvin based his opposition to evolution on the theory of thermodynamics, showing that the earth would have been considerably hotter only one million years ago and any life that lived at that time would have been very different from what can live today. He also showed that these conditions would have produced violent storms and floods over the earth. Also, the second law of thermodynamics, which was developed by four of Kelvin's contemporaries, shows that the natural order of things is to become more disorganized, which clearly contradicts Darwin's theory that living things, over time, become more organized and more complex.

William Thomson, Lord Kelvin, lived an exemplary Christian life. He spent much of his time showing that science supports the idea of an intelligent creator. He wrote, "Mathematics and dynamics fail us when we contemplate the earth, fitted for life but lifeless, and try to imagine the commencement of life upon it. This certainly did not take place by any action of chemistry, or electricity, or crystalline grouping of molecules under the influence of force, or by any possible kind of fortuitous concourse of atoms. We must pause, face to face with the mystery and miracle of the Creation of living creatures." Lord Kelvin believed the Bible when it says that God spoke all life into existence.

Lord Kelvin died on December 17, 1907, in Scotland at the age of 83. He is buried in Westminster Abbey in London, and a stained glass window has been installed in his honor.

Introduction to Chemistry

Measurement of Matter

States of Matter

Classifications of Matter

Solutions

Food Chemistry

Unit Activity & Conclusion

THE METRIC SYSTEM

STANDARD UNITS

SUPPLY LIST:

Measuring cup (metric)   Meter stick
Pencil   Paper clip

Scientists from around the world often work together on projects. In order to do this, they must overcome language barriers and other obstacles. One way scientists overcome the language problem is by using Latin terms whenever possible so there is less confusion. They also use numbers to reduce confusion. Because numbers and quantitative data are so important to science, a standard system for measuring has also been adopted by the scientific community.

The traditional system of measuring used in America is based on the Old English measures established during the Middle Ages. These measurements include the inch, foot, yard, mile, rod, hand and span for length; the ounce, pound and ton for weight/mass; and the fluid ounce, cup, pint, quart and gallon for liquid volume. Because the conversion between units are difficult to use and remember in the Old English/American system, the scientific community has adopted the metric system. The metric system is often referred to as SI units from the term *Système International* (or International System).

The metric system is very easy to use and to remember. All conversions from one unit to another are multiples of 10, so the math is easy. Each type of measurement is based on a standard unit. These units include the meter for length (hence the name metric system), the liter for liquid volume and the gram for mass. The metric unit for time is the second; for temperature it is degrees Kelvin; and for electrical current it is the ampere. If you wish to measure something that is significantly smaller than the standard unit you use a unit that is the standard unit divided by 10 or 100 or some other

GOD'S DESIGN FOR CHEMISTRY
PROPERTIES OF MATTER

Introduction to Chemistry

Measurement of Matter

States of Matter

Classifications of Matter

Solutions

Food Chemistry

Unit Activity & Conclusion

multiple of 10. For example, to measure the length of a paper clip you would use a unit that is a meter divided by 100—a centimeter. To measure something that is significantly larger than the standard you would use a unit that is that standard unit times some multiple of 10. For example, to measure the mass of a paper clip you can use a gram. But to measure the mass of a person you would want to use a unit that is 1000 times bigger than a gram, called a kilogram.

PREFIXES AND CONVERSIONS FOR METRIC UNITS

X1,000,000
mega
(M)

X1000
kilo (k)

X 100
hecto (h)

X 10
deka
(da)

Basic
Unit
meter (m)
gram (g)
liter (l)

1/10
deci (d)

1/100
centi (c)

1/1000
milli (m)

1/1,000,000
micro (μ)

This chart demonstrates how the metric system works. The appropriate prefix is applied to the name of the basic unit. For example 1000 meters is a kilometer and 1000 grams is a kilogram. The symbol in parentheses shows the abbreviation used for that unit. For example a centimeter is abbreviated cm and a kilometer is shown as km. At first, using metric units may seem strange because they are different from what you are used to, but after you use them for a while, you will find that they are much easier to use than the Old English/American units. Besides, it will help you to understand what other scientists are talking about.

USING METRIC UNITS:

To become more familiar with the terminology of the metric system, do

GOD'S DESIGN FOR CHEMISTRY
PROPERTIES OF MATTER

Introduction to Chemistry

Measurement of Matter

States of Matter

Classifications of Matter

Solutions

Food Chemistry

Unit Activity & Conclusion

each of the following activities:

1. Take a giant step—that is about equal to a meter. Now start at one side of the room and measure how many giant steps it takes to cross the room. That is close to how many meters it is from one wall to another. Use a meter stick to get a more accurate measurement after you have walked the distance.

2. Use your hands to show how big a soda pop bottle is. Most bottles of soda are 2 liters. Now show how big half a bottle of pop would be. This is about 1 liter. Try to find a container that holds approximately 1 liter of liquid. Verify the container's volume if you have a measuring cup marked in milliliters or liters.

3. Hold a paper clip in your hand. A small paper clip is about ½ gram. Now hold a pencil. How does a pencil compare to a paper clip? (It is heavier.) How many grams to you think a pencil is? (It depends on the size of the pencil, but could be about 5-10 grams.)

4. For older children with sufficient math skills: use the chart on the previous page to answer the following questions.

    a. If you pour 1000 ml of water into a bottle, how many liters of water do you have?

    b. If you weigh 20 kg, how many grams do you weigh?

    c. If it is 40 hectometers from your house to your best friend's house, how many meters must you walk to get from your house to his?

    d. If your pet hamster is 30 mm long, how long is she in cm?

    e. If you have 5 dekagrams of chocolate to share, how many decigrams do you have?

Answers: a. 1 liter, b. 20,000 grams c. 4000 meters d. 3 centimeters e. 500 decigrams

WHAT DID WE LEARN?

What are some units used to measure length in the Old English/American measuring system? (Inch, foot, yard, mile, rod, hand, span)

What is the unit used to measure length in the metric system? (Meter)

What metric unit is used for measuring mass? (Gram)

What metric unit is used for measuring liquid volume? (Liter)

Why do scientists use the metric system instead of another measuring system? (It is easy to convert from one unit to another and it is based on only a few basic units. In fact, liters and grams are actually based on the meter. For example, the liter is actually the volume of a cube that is .1 X .1 X .1 meters and a gram is the mass of 1/1000 of a liter, or one cubic centimeter, of water.)

GOD'S DESIGN FOR CHEMISTRY
PROPERTIES OF MATTER

Introduction to Chemistry

Measurement of Matter

States of Matter

Classifications of Matter

Solutions

Food Chemistry

Unit Activity & Conclusion

TAKING IT FURTHER

What metric unit would be best to use to measure the distance across a room? (Meters would be the best unit.)

What metric unit would you use to measure the distance from one town to another? (The distance would be a very large number if you used meters, so kilometers would be a better choice.)

What metric unit would you use to measure the width of a hair? (This is much smaller than a meter, so a millimeter or micrometer would be a better choice.)

FUN FACT

The origin of the Old English units is very interesting. In the Middle Ages, an inch was equal to the length of three barley seeds placed end to end. And a yard was equal to the distance from the tip of the king's nose to the end of his outstretched hand. As you can imagine, these lengths varied from time to time so they were never quite accurate. However, the units we use in America today no longer vary with the size of a barley seed of the size of a king. Instead, we have standard measurements. The information necessary for verifying these standard measurements is provided by the National Institute of Standards and Technology (NIST) in Boulder, Colorado. NIST develops and supplies references that companies and other organizations use to check the accuracy of their equipment.

FUN FACT

A meter was originally defined as 1/1,000,000 of the distance from the North Pole to the equator. But it has been redefined to be 1,650,763.73 times the wavelength of light given off by the element Krypton-86.

Introduction to Chemistry Quiz

Lessons 1-4

Number the steps of the scientific method in correct order:

A. _____ Ask a question.

B. _____ Learn about something/Make observations.

C. _____ Share your results.

D. _____ Design a test and perform it.

E. _____ Make an hypothesis.

F. _____ Check your results/Is your hypothesis right?

Answer True or False for each statement.

1. _____ You must always have a correct hypothesis.

2. _____ It is important to control variables in your experiments.

3. _____ Qualitative measurements always use numbers.

4. _____ Quantitative measurements can be more useful to scientists than qualitative measurements.

5. _____ It is usually easier to make conversions between units in the metric system than in the Old English/American system.

6. _____ A millimeter is smaller than a meter.

7. _____ A graduated cylinder should be used to measure mass.

8. _____ God has established laws to govern how chemicals react with each other.

9. _____ Science can always tell us why things happen.

10. _____ Air is invisible so it has no mass.

Describe what Chemistry is the study of. _____

_____

(Note: answers to all quizzes and tests are in Appendix A)

Introduction to Chemistry

Measurement of Matter

States of Matter

Classifications of Matter

Solutions

Food Chemistry

Unit Activity & Conclusion

LESSON 5

MASS VERSUS WEIGHT

WHAT'S THE DIFFERENCE?

SUPPLY LIST:

Ruler	Thin rubber band
String	2 pencils
3 paper cups	Paper
25 pennies	Tape
Several paper clips	Single hole punch

When studying matter, one of the first questions scientists ask is, "How much matter do we have?" The amount of matter in a sample is called its mass. The mass of an object does not depend on its shape. If you start with a ball of Silly Putty and you flatten it into a disk you still have the same amount of Silly Putty. You have not changed its mass. You have not changed how much you have.

People often confuse weight with mass. Mass is how much of something there is. Weight is a measure of how strongly one thing is attracted to another by gravity. On earth, weight is a measure of how much the earth pulls on an object, such as your body. Because the gravitational pull on earth is defined as 1, the weight of an object and its mass are the same on earth. But in space, where there is no gravity, a person becomes weightless but his/her mass remains the same.

Mass is measured by using a balance to compare an object's mass with a known mass. You place the object to be measured on one side of the balance and known masses on the other side of the balance until both sides are even. For example, to measure the mass of a pencil, you would place it on one side of a balance, and then add 1-gram mass pieces to the other side until both sides are balanced. This would show you the mass of the pencil.

Because weight is a measurement of gravitational pull, it is measured

GOD'S DESIGN FOR CHEMISTRY
PROPERTIES OF MATTER

Introduction
to Chemistry

Measurement
of Matter

States of Matter

Classifications
of Matter

Solutions

Food Chemistry

Unit Activity
& Conclusion

using a spring scale. The object to be measured is attached to one end of a spring and the other end is held up. The amount that the spring stretches indicates the weight of the object. With many spring scales the object can be placed on top of a spring and the amount the spring compresses shows the object's weight. This is how most bathroom scales work.

In SI units, mass is measured using grams for small objects such as an eraser or a cherry, and kilograms (1000 grams) for larger objects such as people or cars. The metric system unit for weight is the Newton—named after Sir Isaac Newton.

So even though we often use the terms weight and mass interchangeably, there is a difference. Mass is how much material you have, and weight is how much gravity pulls down on that material.

MEASURING MASS AND WEIGHT:

To measure mass you need to build a balance. This can be done by following the steps below:

1. If you have a ruler with a hole in it, you can put a pencil through the hole. Otherwise, securely tape a pencil to the center of the ruler.

2. Punch a hole near the top of a paper cup. Punch a second hole directly across from the first hole. Tie the ends of a 50 cm piece of string to the cup through the holes. Tape the center of the string to the ruler approximately 2 cm from one end.

3. Repeat step 2 and tape the string of the second cup to the other end of the ruler.

4. While holding the pencil, see if the empty cups balance so that the ruler is level. If not, adjust one cup by moving it closer to or further from the center until the balance is level.

Now you can use your balance to find the mass of small objects. Place a small object in one cup. Now place pennies one at a time in the other cup until the ruler is level. A penny has the mass of approximately 3 grams so multiply the number of pennies by 3 to determine the approximate mass of the object. If the object has a mass that is less than that of a penny, you can use paper clips. Small paper clips are about ½ gram each. Save this balance to use in lessons 6 and 8.

To measure the weight of an object you need to build a spring scale. But since springs can be hard to find we will use a rubber band instead.

1. Prepare a cup like you did for the balance by punching holes in it and tying a string to it, but put the

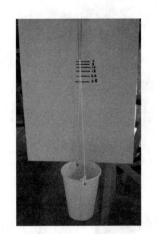

string through a rubber band before tying the second end to the cup.

2. Place a pencil through the rubber band to hold up the top of your scale.

3. Set the pencil on a table near the edge so the scale hangs in front of the table.

4. Tape a piece of paper to the edge of the table so that it is behind the rubber band and cup.

5. Make a mark on the paper showing the bottom of the rubber band when there is nothing in the cup.

6. Place five pennies in the cup and mark the bottom of the rubber band on the paper.

7. Repeat this for 10 pennies, 15 pennies, 20 pennies and 25 pennies, marking where the bottom of the rubber band is at each measurement.

8. Remove the pennies. Now your spring scale is ready to use.

Place a small object in the cup and see how much it stretches the rubber band. You can compare this to the weight of the pennies. Because weight and mass are equal on earth, you can compare the results you get with the scale to those you get with the balance.

WHAT DID WE LEARN?

What is the difference between mass and weight? (Mass is the amount of material there is in an object and weight is how much gravity pulls down on an object.)

How do you measure mass? (By using a balance to compare an object to a known mass)

How do you measure weight? (By using a spring scale that is marked for known weights)

Where is the only known place in the universe that weight and mass are equal? (On earth)

TAKING IT FURTHER

What would your weight be in outer space? (Zero, or nearly zero because there is very little gravity in space.)

What would your mass be in outer space? (The same as it is on earth)

Name a place in the universe where you might go to increase your weight without changing your mass. (Any of the larger planets such as Jupiter or Saturn. Of course, you cannot really go there and you could not survive there if you could, but the gravity is much higher there than on earth so you would weigh much more there.)

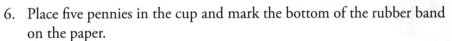

GOD'S DESIGN FOR CHEMISTRY
PROPERTIES OF MATTER

Introduction to Chemistry

Measurement of Matter

States of Matter

Classifications of Matter

Solutions

Food Chemistry

Unit Activity & Conclusion

Introduction
to Chemistry

Measurement
of Matter

States of Matter

Classifications
of Matter

Solutions

Food Chemistry

Unit Activity
& Conclusion

CONSERVATION OF MASS

WHERE DOES IT GO?

LESSON

6

SUPPLY LIST:

2 paper cups
2 sugar cubes

Balance from lesson 5

In the previous lesson you learned that mass is how much of a substance is in a sample or object. You may think that mass changes when something changes form because it looks different or it takes up a different amount of space, but this is not true. For example, lets say you have 10 grams of water in a cup. That water can change form, it can be frozen and become ice, or it can be boiled and become steam, but you will still have 10 grams of water. Similarly, if you have a 20 gram rock and you hit it with a hammer until it is broken into tiny pieces, you will still have 20 grams of rock. The pieces will be very small but if you put them all together the mass remains the same.

Sometimes matter doesn't just change form; sometimes it combines with other matter to make a new substance. Hydrogen and oxygen molecules combine to form water. But if you have 100 grams of hydrogen and oxygen before they combine, you will have 100 grams of water after. In general, the amount of mass does not change even in a chemical reaction. Occasionally, a chemical reaction does produce a slightly smaller amount of mass because some mass has been converted into energy.

The fact that matter does not go away is a law called the Law of Conservation of Mass. Energy also does not go away and this fact is called the Law of Conservation of Energy. These two laws taken together are called the 1st Law of Thermodynamics. This law states, "Matter and energy cannot be created nor destroyed, they can only change form." The Law of Conservation of Mass is very important and is apparent all around us. The water cycle is God's way of providing for our needs. Water evaporates from the oceans, lakes and rivers. It then forms into clouds and eventually falls as rain or other precipitation to provide water for crops and people. If water was used up in this process the world would eventually run out of water.

Another example of the conservation of mass occurs in plants. Plants absorb nutrients such as nitrogen from the ground. Then when they die, they decay and return those nutrients to the soil. An animal may eat the plant and absorb the nutrients into its body, but when the animal dies, it decays and returns the nutrients to the soil to be used by other plants. This reusing of nutrients is part of the conservation of mass. It is God's way of recycling so that we do not run out of essential materials.

The Law of Conservation of Mass raises an important question. If matter cannot be created nor destroyed, then where did it come from in the first place? This is a question that cannot be answered by operational science. The Bible tells us in Genesis chapter 1 that God spoke the universe into existence. This is the only viable explanation for the matter that exists today. God created it and it continues to exist because man cannot destroy it. God set up a wonderful system to maintain life on earth through the reusing of all matter on the planet.

Changing Form Without Losing Mass:

To help you understand that changing the form of something does not change its mass, perform the following experiment.

In a paper cup, dissolve a sugar cube in a small amount of water. Where did the sugar go? (It is still there, in the water. It just looks different because it has been broken into very small pieces by the water molecules.)

Set the cup in a place where it will not be disturbed. Check the cup every day until all of the water is evaporated. What do you see in the bottom of the cup? (You should see sugar crystals.)

Set up the balance you made in lesson 5. Place the cup with the sugar crystals in the cup on one side of the balance and place a second identical cup with one sugar cube in it in the other cup of the balance. Do both cups balance? (They should.) This shows that the sugar cube did not go away when it was dissolved in the water. It just changed form into crystals instead of a cube, but it still has the same mass.

What did we learn?

What does the Law of Conservation of Mass say? (Matter cannot be created nor destroyed. It can change form, but it does not go away.)

How is the mass of water changed when it turns to ice? (It does not change.)

Taking it further

If you start with 10 grams of water and you boil it until there is no water left in the pan, what happened to the water? (The 10 grams of water

Introduction to Chemistry

Measurement of Matter

States of Matter

Classifications of Matter

Solutions

Food Chemistry

Unit Activity & Conclusion

Introduction to Chemistry

Measurement of Matter

States of Matter

Classifications of Matter

Solutions

Food Chemistry

Unit Activity & Conclusion

turned into 10 grams of steam and entered the air, but it did not disappear or go away.)

Why is the Law of Conservation of Mass important to understanding the beginning of the world? (It shows that matter cannot create itself or be created by anything in nature. Therefore it had to be created by something outside of nature. We know from the Bible that all matter was created by God.)

Introduction to Chemistry

Measurement of Matter

States of Matter

Classifications of Matter

Solutions

Food Chemistry

Unit Activity & Conclusion

VOLUME

HOW MUCH SPACE DOES IT TAKE UP?

LESSON 7

SUPPLY LIST:

Meter stick
Metric ruler
Liquid measuring cup

Small box
Small object (eraser, toy, etc.)

When scientists study matter they make many measurements to help them understand more about the material they are studying. They measure mass so they know how much matter they have. They also measure volume.

Volume is how much space the matter takes up. For example, if you want to know how much room you need to stack boxes in a warehouse, you would need to know the volume of each box or how much room it takes up. If a box is 10 cm wide, 15 cm long and 2 cm high it has a volume of 300 cubic centimeters (10 X 15 X 2 = 300). You would need to allow 300 cubic centimeters of room for each box you want to store.

Measuring the volume of something solid that has a regular shape like a rectangle, cube or sphere is easy to do. You just need to measure the height, length and width, and then use a little math to calculate the volume. However, scientists work with many materials that are not solids, and many materials that are not regular shapes.

To measure the volume of a liquid, you need a container that has marks on its side. For example, you can measure the volume of water in a liquid measuring

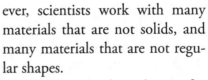

GOD'S DESIGN FOR CHEMISTRY
PROPERTIES OF MATTER

Introduction to Chemistry

Measurement of Matter

States of Matter

Classifications of Matter

Solutions

Food Chemistry

Unit Activity & Conclusion

cup. Scientists usually use beakers or graduated cylinders instead of kitchen measuring cups to make accurate measurements of liquids. The units that scientists use for liquid volume are milliliters (or cubic centimeters). To get a correct measurement of any liquid, you need to set the measuring cup or cylinder on a level surface. Then you need to get down so your eye is level with the liquid. This will allow you to correctly read the amount of liquid in the container. If you are using a graduated cylinder or other device that is relatively narrow, the liquid may be slightly higher on the sides than in the center like the picture shown here. This curve is called a meniscus, and you should use the lowest point of the meniscus as your measurement.

To measure the volume of a gas, you must measure the volume of its container because gas expands to fill its container. For example, the air in a room fills up the room. In a balloon, the volume of air is equal to the volume of the balloon because the air spreads out to fill the whole balloon.

All of these volume measurements are relatively simple to make. But how do scientists measure the volume of an unusually shaped item like a rock or a toy? To measure the volume of an irregularly shaped object, a scientist fills a graduated cylinder part way with water and notes its volume. Then he/she carefully drops in the object to be measured and notes the new volume. The scientist can then simply subtract the first measurement from the second to determine the volume of the object. This is called the displacement method. For example, if the cylinder originally has 25 milliliters (ml) of water in it, and then an eraser is dropped in and the water level goes up to 47 ml, the volume of the eraser is 22 ml (47 ml – 25 ml). Note that the original amount of water must be enough to completely cover the object that is being measured.

If an object is too big to fit in a graduated cylinder, the overflow method can be used. To do this, set a container that is big enough to hold the object inside a dish or tray. Then fill the container completely full of water. Carefully drop the object into the water, allowing the water to overflow into the dish. Carefully pour the water that overflowed into a graduated cylinder and measure its volume. The volume of the water that overflowed is equal to the volume of the object.

As you can see, there are many ways to measure how much room something takes up.

MEASURING VOLUME:

Practice finding the volume of several objects.

1. Measure the volume of a small box. Use a metric ruler to measure the length, width and height of the box in centimeters. Multiply these three numbers together to obtain the volume of the box in cubic centimeters.
2. Measure the volume of water that a glass can hold. Fill a glass with water, then carefully pour the water into a liquid measuring cup.

GOD'S DESIGN FOR CHEMISTRY · PROPERTIES OF MATTER

Introduction to Chemistry

Measurement of Matter

States of Matter

Classifications of Matter

Solutions

Food Chemistry

Unit Activity & Conclusion

Be sure to place the measuring cup on a level surface and bend down until your eye is even with the water level to determine the volume of the water. Your measuring cup may use ounces, cups or milliliters as its units.

3. Measure the volume of air in your school room. Use a meter stick to measure the length, width and height of your room. Multiply these numbers together to determine the volume of the room in cubic meters. This is not quite equal to the volume of air because you are in the room and you probably have furniture and other items in the room that are taking up space. But it tells you the volume of air that would be in the room if the room were empty.

4. Determine the volume of an irregularly shaped object. If you have an object that is small enough to fit in the measuring cup, use the displacement method to determine its volume. If you want to measure something that does not fit in the cup, use the overflow method described in the lesson.

WHAT DID WE LEARN?

What is volume? (The amount of room or space something occupies.)

Does air have volume? (Yes, even though you can't see it, it still takes up space. It expands to fill up the available space. Think about a balloon. The air forces the balloon to expand; visibly showing how much room the air is taking up.)

TAKING IT FURTHER

If you have a cube that is 10 centimeters on each side, what would its volume be? (10 cm X 10 cm X 10 cm = 1000 cubic centimeters.)

Why is volume important to a scientist? (The volume of matter can be related to many things that scientists are interested in. For example, the volume that a certain amount of fuel occupies determines how a vehicle will be designed.)

FUN FACT

For those of you who are math whizzes, here are some mathematical formulas for helping you calculate the volume of certain shapes:

Volume of a cube = Side X Side X Side
Volume of a rectangle = Length X Width X Height
Volume of a sphere = (4/3) π Radius X Radius X Radius
$\qquad$ Where π = approximately 3.14
Volume of a cylinder = π Radius X Radius X Height
Volume of a cone = (1/3) π Radius X Radius X Height

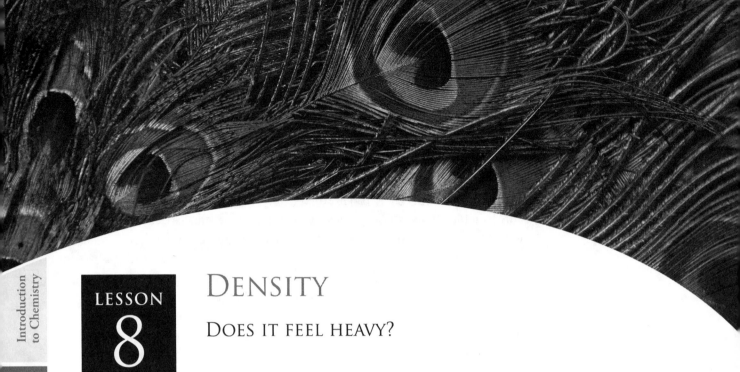

Introduction to Chemistry

Measurement of Matter

States of Matter

Classifications of Matter

Solutions

Food Chemistry

Unit Activity & Conclusion

LESSON 8

DENSITY

DOES IT FEEL HEAVY?

SUPPLY LIST:

Ping-pong ball
Golf ball
Balance from lesson 5

Have you ever held a ping-pong ball in one hand and a golf ball in the other? Even though the balls have nearly the same volume—they take up about the same amount of space—the golf ball is heavier than the ping-pong ball. This is because the golf ball has more mass in the same area. It is more dense.

Density is the relationship between mass and volume. Density is defined as the mass divided by the volume. Here is another example to help you understand density. Which has more mass, a kilogram of feathers or a kilogram of lead? You may have answered that a kilogram of lead has more mass because we usually think of lead as being heavy and feathers as being light. But a kilogram of lead is the same amount of mass as a kilogram of feathers. However, the pile of feathers would be much larger—it would have a greater volume—than the pile of lead. Lead is very dense. A cubic centimeter of lead is 11.3 grams. But feathers are much less dense. There is less than 1 gram of feathers in a cubic centimeter of feathers. Because density is defined as mass divided by volume its units are usually given as grams/milliliter or grams/cubic centimeter.

Understanding density is important to scientists for many reasons. One use of density is to help the scientist determine what a sample of material is made of. If someone were interested in opening a mine, they would take samples of ore found in the area to a scientist to determine what metals are present. One way the scientist determines what metals are present is to measure the sample's density. Different metals have different densities.

GOD'S DESIGN FOR CHEMISTRY
PROPERTIES OF MATTER

Introduction to Chemistry

Measurement of Matter

States of Matter

Classifications of Matter

Solutions

Food Chemistry

Unit Activity & Conclusion

Gold is very dense so it feels heavier than a similar sized piece of copper, which has a much lower density. If the ore has a density close to 9 g/cc it is likely to contain copper, and if it has a density close to 19 g/cc it is likely to contain gold.

Another reason that scientists are interested in density is to determine how a material might be used. If something is very dense it is more ideal for some uses than others. If it has a low density it may be more useful in other areas. For example, fiberglass and styrofoam are materials that are not very dense because they have tiny air pockets trapped inside. This property makes them very good insulators. Fiberglass insulation is used to keep many houses warm in the winter and styrofoam cups keep you from burning your hands when you hold a cup of hot chocolate. Many objects that are more dense, such as metals, conduct heat and do not make good insulators.

MEASURING DENSITY:

Determine the density of a ping-pong ball by doing the following:

1. Measure the mass of the ball using your balance and pennies or paper clips.

2. Measure the volume of the ball using the water displacement method from lesson 7. If the ball floats, carefully push the ball just under the surface of the water with your finger.

3. Divide the mass by the volume to determine the ball's density.

Repeat these three steps to determine the density of a golf ball.

How did the mass of the golf ball compare to the mass of the ping-pong ball? (It should be significantly more.)

How did the volume of the golf ball compare to the volume of the ping-pong ball? (It should be about the same.)

Which ball has a higher density? (The golf ball)

WHAT DID WE LEARN?

What is the definition of density? (The mass of an object divided by its volume.)

If two substances with the same volume have different densities how can you tell which one is the densest? (If they have the same volume, the one that is heavier will have the higher density.)

TAKING IT FURTHER

If you have two unknown substances that both appear to be silvery colored, how can you tell if they are the same material? (Measure their densities. Platinum has a density of 21.45 g/cc, lead is 11.3 g/cc and aluminum is 2.7 g/cc. This may give you a clue to the material's identity.)

If two objects have the same density and the same size what will be true

GOD'S DESIGN FOR CHEMISTRY
PROPERTIES OF MATTER

Introduction
to Chemistry

Measurement
of Matter

States of Matter

Classifications
of Matter

Solutions

Food Chemistry

Unit Activity
& Conclusion

about their masses? (They will have the same mass.)

If you suspect that someone is trying to pass off a gold plated bar of lead as a solid gold bar, how can you test your theory? (Measure the density of the bar. Gold has a density of 19.3 g/cc while lead has a density of 11.3 g/cc. Even though lead may seem heavy, it is not as dense as gold.)

Why does the ping-pong ball have a lower density than the golf ball? (It is filled with air. Air is very light compared to most substances. The golf ball is filled with plastic, rubber or other solid materials.)

FUN FACT

The densest known substance on earth is osmium. Osmium has a density of 22.48 grams/cubic centimeter.

FUN FACT

The early miners in the California gold rush used the fact that gold is very dense to help them pan for gold. Because gold is very heavy compared to other substances in the riverbed, it sank to the bottom of the mining pan, while other lighter substances were washed away by the water.

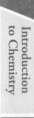

Introduction to Chemistry

Measurement of Matter

States of Matter

Classifications of Matter

Solutions

Food Chemistry

Unit Activity & Conclusion

LESSON

9

BUOYANCY

IT FLOATS!

SUPPLY LIST:

Rubbing alcohol   Vegetable oil
Modeling clay   2 cups
Popcorn (including some unpopped kernels)

Have you ever wondered how something as heavy as a battleship can float on the water when a small rock sinks when you toss it in a lake? The ability of matter to float is called buoyancy and is directly related to its density. An object that is denser than its surroundings will sink while an object that is less dense will float. If the object floats it is said to be buoyant or to have buoyancy.

So why is a battleship more buoyant than a rock? The battleship is less dense than the rock. Even though the ship has much more mass than the rock, it is shaped so that is has a much greater volume. And most of the ship's volume is filled with air, which is much lighter and less dense than water. Thus the ship's overall density is less than the density of the water and so it floats. A rock, however, has a small mass and a small volume. Thus it has a higher density than the water, so it sinks. A few rocks have low densities and can float on the water.

You have probably used the principle of buoyancy when you were swimming. When you take a deep breath you are able to float because the air in your lungs decreases your overall density—increasing your buoyancy. Your body becomes less dense than the water so you are able to float.

Not all solids have the same density and not all liquids have the same density. For example, Mercury is a very dense liquid and would quickly sink to the bottom of a glass of water. You would never go swimming in a pool of mercury, but if you could, you would have no problem floating on the surface. However, if you went swimming in a pool of rubbing alcohol you

GOD'S DESIGN FOR CHEMISTRY
PROPERTIES OF MATTER

Introduction
to Chemistry

Measurement
of Matter

States of Matter

Classifications
of Matter

Solutions

Food Chemistry

Unit Activity
& Conclusion

would have a very difficult time keeping your head above the surface because alcohol is less dense than water and you would no longer be buoyant.

So you can see that buoyancy is relative. It is the difference in the density of one substance compared to another. One of the most important applications of buoyancy is the fact that frozen water is less dense than liquid water so ice floats on liquid water. Water is the only known substance that becomes less dense when it becomes a solid. This was a special design by God. If ice did not float, but instead sank to the bottom of the lake, the lakes and ponds would all freeze solid in the wintertime and life would quickly die in them. So give thanks to God for making ice buoyant!

TESTING BUOYANCY:

Perform the following tests to observe buoyancy.

Solid in a liquid:
Take two equal size pieces of modeling clay. Roll one into a solid ball. Shape the second piece into a flat bottomed boat shape. Place both pieces of clay in a sink filled with water. Which shape floats? (If you formed the boat carefully, you should be able to get it to float, whereas the ball will probably sink.)

Solid in a solid:
Pop some popcorn and put it in a bowl. Be sure to include several unpopped kernels. Mix the popcorn up with the kernels. Now gently shake the bowl for a few seconds. What did you observe happening? (You should see the fluffy pieces rise to the top and the unpopped kernels sink to the bottom. The kernels are denser than the popped pieces. The popped pieces take up more space, but have the same amount of matter as the kernels so they are less dense and thus rise to the top.)

Liquid in a liquid:
Pour some water in one cup and some rubbing alcohol in a second cup. Pour a small amount of vegetable oil in each cup. What happened to the oil in each cup? (You should have observed that the oil floated on the top of the water but sank to the bottom of the alcohol.) Why did the oil float in one cup but sink in the other? (Oil is less dense than water but more dense than alcohol. The oil is buoyant in the water but not in the alcohol.)

WHAT DID WE LEARN?

What is buoyancy? (The ability to float.)

If something is buoyant, what does that tell you about its density compared to that of the substance in which it floats? (It means that the object's density is less than the density of the substance that it is floating on.)

Are you buoyant in water? (Probably, especially if you are holding your breath.)

GOD'S DESIGN FOR CHEMISTRY
PROPERTIES OF MATTER

Introduction to Chemistry

Measurement of Matter

States of Matter

Classifications of Matter

Solutions

Food Chemistry

Unit Activity & Conclusion

TAKING IT FURTHER

What are some substances that are buoyant in water besides you? (Ivory soap, a leaf, paper, oil, etc.)

Based on what you observed, which is denser, water or alcohol? (Water is denser. Oil will float on the water but sinks in the alcohol.)

Why is a foam swimming tube or a foam life ring able to keep a person afloat in the water? (Foam is a material that has air trapped in it so it is not very dense. Even with the person's weight/mass added to it, the foam object's density remains lower than the density of the water.)

Why is it important to life that ice is less dense than water? (Otherwise rivers and lakes would freeze from the bottom up, and no life could survive in them.)

FUN FACT

Nuclear powered submarines must be bigger than diesel powered submarines in order to be buoyant. This is because nuclear reactors are much heavier than diesel engines. Therefore, the nuclear submarine must have a greater volume filled with air to compensate for the additional mass of the reactor in order to be buoyant in the water.

James Clerk Maxwell

(1831-1879)

Math, science, nature and Christianity; what do these things all have in common? They were all important in the life of James Clerk Maxwell. Maxwell, described as one of the outstanding mathematicians and scientists of the 19th century, was born in Edinburgh, Scotland. He was an only child and was home educated by his mother until her death in 1838. After spending 2 years with a tutor, James attended Edinburgh Academy, where he graduated at the top of his class in english and math. He then attended the University of Edinburgh and continued his studies at Trinity College.

After he completed his training, Maxwell spent some time teaching at Marischal College, where met and married Katherine Mary Dewar, the daughter of the college principle. He later became the professor of physics and astronomy at Kings College in London, and in 1871, he became the Chair of Experimental Physics at Cambridge University.

Although Maxwell spent time teaching at each of these schools, his real interest was in experimenting and testing out new ideas. Maxwell was the first to explain the kinetic theory of gases, showing that the movement of gas particles creates heat and pressure. He also tested the viscosity, or density, of gases. He was the first to suggest that the rings around Saturn were not a solid or a gas, but a collection of millions of tiny particles that orbit the planet. This idea was proven to be true when the Voyager 1 space probe visited Saturn in 1980. It sent back pictures showing that the rings are composed of millions of pieces of ice, dust and rocks.

Maxwell is best known for his work in electromagnetism. He worked closely with Michael Faraday, and helped to mathematically describe the electromagnetic fields that generate electricity. Today, these equations are called Maxwell's Equations. Born out of his work with electricity, Maxwell advanced the idea that light was a form of electromagnetic energy.

Despite all his scientific work, the people closest to Maxwell did not describe him as a great scientist. Instead, they described him has a humble, godly man. James was an elder in his church and he fervently believed that the reason to study nature was to draw people to God so they could ultimately have a saving relationship with the Creator. Maxwell died of cancer at the age of 48. He left behind a great scientific legacy, but more importantly, he left behind a legacy of humble obedience to God.

MEASUREMENT OF MATTER QUIZ

LESSONS 5-9

Matching – draw a line from the phrase to the word it describes

1.	The amount of a substance	conservation of mass
2.	How strongly something is pulled on by gravity	density
3.	Matter cannot be created or destroyed	mass
4.	How much space matter occupies	volume
5.	How much mass is in a particular volume	spring scale
6.	The ability for one substance to float in another	balance
7.	Used to measure mass	buoyancy
8.	Used to measure weight	weight
9.	A material that is denser than lead	water
10.	Only material to become less dense when frozen	gold

Short answer.

11. Explain how the water you drink today could be the same water a dinosaur drank thousands of years ago._____

_____

12. Explain what happens to nitrogen in the soil and in plants that demonstrates conservation of mass. _____

_____

13. If an object floats in one liquid but sinks in another, what does that tell you about the densities of the two liquids? _____

14. How would you determine the volume of a toy car? _____

_____

15. How are buoyancy and density related? _____

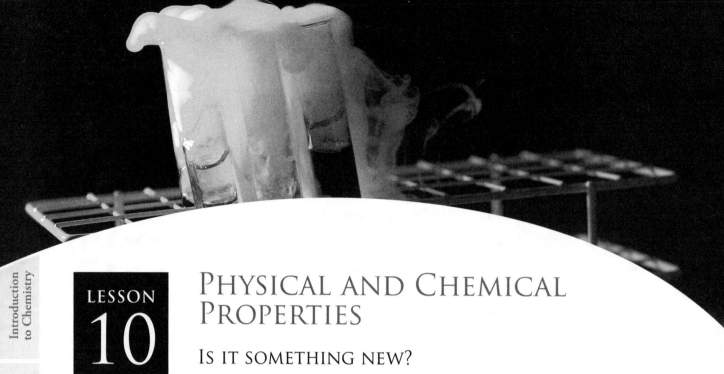

Introduction
to Chemistry

Measurement
of Matter

States of Matter

Classifications
of Matter

Solutions

Food Chemistry

Unit Activity
& Conclusion

LESSON 10

PHYSICAL AND CHEMICAL PROPERTIES

IS IT SOMETHING NEW?

SUPPLY LIST:

1 copy of "Physical or Chemical Properties" per child (pg. 38)

As we learned in the first lesson, chemistry is the study of matter and how it reacts to the things around it. We know that scientists use tools and make measurements to study matter. When scientists, particularly chemists, study matter they investigate both the physical and chemical properties of the matter.

A physical property is one that can be measured, studied and tested without changing what kind of matter is being studied. We have already learned about some physical properties including mass, volume, density and buoyancy. Other physical properties include color, texture and hardness. All of these characteristics can be measured or observed without changing one substance into another substance.

This does not mean that the matter does not change form. A substance can experience a physical change without becoming a different substance. For example, when liquid water freezes it becomes ice but it is still water. Dry ice becomes a gas as it warms up but it is still carbon dioxide. Also, the shape of a substance can be changed without changing what substance it is, like when a rubber band stretches. It has a different shape, but it is still a rubber band. If a sugar cube is ground into powered sugar it has a different physical form, but it is still sugar. All of these changes in shape and state are physical changes and are one way that chemists study matter.

But another way that chemists study matter is by testing its chemical properties. Chemical properties describe how a substance reacts in the presence of other substances to create new substances. Remember when you put vinegar and baking soda together? It foamed and produced gas bubbles. This is a chemical property of the vinegar and soda. They combined to form carbon dioxide. Chemical reactions change the identity of the substances.

One of the most important chemical changes designed by God is photosynthesis. In photosynthesis water and carbon dioxide are changed by sunlight into sugar and oxygen through a chemical reaction. This chemical change provides food for nearly every living thing on earth.

So become a good chemist and learn to detect chemical and physical changes in the matter around you.

PHYSICAL VS. CHEMICAL CHANGES:

Complete the "Physical or Chemical Properties" worksheet.

Answers: 1. P, 2. Primarily C (P – texture contributes to taste), 3. C, 4. P, 5. P, 6. P, 7. C, 8. P, 9. P, 10. C, 11. C, 12. P, 13. C, 14. C, 15. P, 16. C 17. P 18. C, 19. P, 20. C

WHAT DID WE LEARN?

What are some physical properties of matter? (These could include color, texture, temperature, density, mass, state, etc.)

What is a chemical change? (When two or more substances combine to form a different substance.)

Give an example of a chemical change. (There are innumerable examples. Some common chemical changes that might be mentioned include photosynthesis, hydrogen and oxygen combining to form water, vinegar and baking soda combining to form carbon dioxide, yeast turning sugar into carbon dioxide, rust, digesting food, etc.)

TAKING IT FURTHER

How can you determine if a change in matter is a physical change or a chemical change? (Find out if the ending matter is the same type of matter as what you started with.)

Diamond and quartz may appear to have very similar physical properties. They are both clear crystalline substances. However, diamond is much harder than quartz. How would this affect their effectiveness as tips for drill bits? (The quartz-tipped drill would quickly wear down and be ineffective. Diamond-tipped drills are very hard and very effective at drilling through nearly any other substance. It is important to understand physical properties of matter as well as chemical properties.)

PHYSICAL OR CHEMICAL PROPERTIES

For each change listed below write P if it describes a physical change or physical property, and C if it describes a chemical change or chemical property. To determine if it is a chemical change, ask yourself if a new substance is being formed.

1. _____ Liquid water becoming steam

2. _____ Flavor/taste

3. _____ Burning of wood/fire

4. _____ Filling a balloon with air

5. _____ Softness

6. _____ Making ice cream

7. _____ Digesting food

8. _____ Straightening a paper clip

9. _____ Cloud formation

10. _____ Rust on a piece of iron

11. _____ Separation of water into hydrogen and oxygen gases

12. _____ Dissolving sugar in water

13. _____ Photosynthesis

14. _____ Bacteria decaying dead plant matter

15. _____ Shine/luster

16. _____ A cake rising in the oven

17. _____ Cutting a piece of wood

18. _____ Bread rising

19. _____ Hardness

20. _____ Making perfume

(Answers are on page 37)

Introduction to Chemistry

Measurement of Matter

States of Matter

Classifications of Matter

Solutions

Food Chemistry

Unit Activity & Conclusion

LESSON 11

STATES OF MATTER

PHASE CHANGES

SUPPLY LIST:

Ice
Hand mirror

Small saucepan
Ice tray

All matter has physical and chemical properties. One physical property of a substance is its physical state. When we speak of physical state we are talking about whether the substance is a gas, a liquid or a solid. A substance's physical state is determined by how tightly its molecules cling to each other and the amount of energy necessary to make the molecules move apart.

In a solid, the molecules are packed tightly together and do not move very much. They are strongly attracted to each other. As energy, usually in the form of heat, is added to the substance, the molecules begin to move; their kinetic energy increases. Kinetic energy is the energy of motion or moving particles. As more heat is added, the molecules eventually gain enough energy to move away from each other. When the forces pulling them together equal the forces pushing them apart, the substance changes from a solid to a liquid.

If more energy is added to the liquid, the molecules move even faster. Eventually they gain enough energy to break free of the other molecules and became a gas. In a gas, the molecules are far

GOD'S DESIGN FOR CHEMISTRY
PROPERTIES OF MATTER

Introduction to Chemistry

Measurement of Matter

States of Matter

Classifications of Matter

Solutions

Food Chemistry

Unit Activity & Conclusion

apart from each other and move very quickly.

Similarly, if molecules lose energy, if heat is transferred to something else like cooler air, the molecules will slow down. A gas will become a liquid or a liquid will become a solid when it loses enough energy for the molecules to become attracted to each other again.

When a substance changes from one physical state to another it is called a phase change. When a solid becomes a liquid we say that is has melted. The temperature at which the substance melts is called the melting point. When a liquid becomes a gas it has evaporated. The temperature at which a liquid begins to evaporate is called the boiling point. When a gas becomes a liquid it has condensed, and when a liquid becomes a solid we say it has frozen.

Some substances can change directly from a solid into a gas or directly from a gas into a solid without going through a liquid phase. This phase

change is called sublimation. Two of the most common substances that experience sublimation are carbon dioxide and mothballs. Dry ice, shown here, is frozen carbon dioxide. When it is placed in a warm environment it quickly sublimates directly into a gas without leaving any liquid behind. This makes it very popular in the food industry for keeping foods frozen while being transported.

The vast majority of substances on earth are solids at normal temperature and pressure. Water is one very important substance that occurs in all three states, depending on the weather. And several substances, including oxygen and nitrogen naturally occur as gases on earth. The fact that the earth is made of substances that are solid is another example of God's provision for life on earth. Many of the planets in our solar system are made of hydrogen and other elements that are naturally gases and would not be able to support life, but earth was designed perfectly for life.

OBSERVING PHASE CHANGES:

1. Observe a piece of ice. How does it feel? (Hard, cold, smooth)

2. Now, place a few pieces of ice in a small saucepan and melt it over medium heat just until most of the ice is melted. Remove the pan from the heat and observe the liquid water. How does the liquid compare to the solid? (It is warmer, can be moved easier, wet)

GOD'S DESIGN FOR CHEMISTRY

PROPERTIES OF MATTER

Introduction to Chemistry

Measurement of Matter

States of Matter

Classifications of Matter

Solutions

Food Chemistry

Unit Activity & Conclusion

3. Return the pan to the stove on medium heat. Watch as the water begins to boil. Be careful not to put your hand in the steam. It could burn. What did you notice as the water began to boil? (Little bubbles came up from the bottom of the pan. Steam rose from the water.)

4. Place a hand mirror in the steam and watch as some of the steam condenses on the mirror. How does the water on the mirror feel? (Cool and wet)

5. Remove the pan from the stove. Pour the water into an ice tray and place the tray in the freezer. After 1-2 hours observe the water again. How does the water look and feel now? (Cold, hard, and smooth.)

You have now seen the phase changes of water. Review the names of each phase change:

Solid to Liquid – Melting
Liquid to Gas – Evaporation
Gas to Liquid – Condensation
Liquid to Solid – Freezing

You did not observe sublimation; the changing of a solid directly to gas or a gas directly to a solid.

WHAT DID WE LEARN?

What are the three physical states of most matter? (Solid, liquid, gas)

What is the name for each phase change? (Solid to liquid is melting, liquid to gas is evaporation, gas to liquid is condensation, liquid to solid is freezing, and for those substances that can go directly from solid to gas or gas to solid, the phase change is called sublimation.)

What is required to bring about a phase change in a substance? (The addition or removal of energy—primarily in the form of heat)

TAKING IT FURTHER

Name several substances that are solid at room temperature. (The answers are endless. Some ideas include metals, wood, plastic, many foods, people, animals, etc.)

Name several substances that are liquid at room temperature. (Some ideas include water, juice, tea, honey, rubbing alcohol and syrup.)

Name several substances that are gas at room temperature. (Some ideas include air, nitrogen, oxygen, hydrogen, carbon dioxide, carbon monoxide, propane and natural gas.)

Introduction to Chemistry

Measurement of Matter

States of Matter

Classifications of Matter

Solutions

Food Chemistry

Unit Activity & Conclusion

LESSON 12

SOLIDS

HARD AS A ROCK.

SUPPLY LIST:

Wooden block
Rock

Honey
Metal spoon

Matter on earth almost always exists in one of three states: solid, liquid or gas. When a substance is a solid, its molecules have very low kinetic energy and are strongly attracted to each other. The molecules move very slowly and only vibrate. This movement is so slow that it is generally not noticeable.

There are several other characteristics that are common to all solids. If you pick up something, how do you know if it is a solid, a liquid or a gas? You might say it is a solid if it is hard or if it is heavy. However, not all solids are hard and not all solids are heavy. A piece of paper is a solid but it is not hard or heavy. So what makes a solid different from a liquid or a gas?

First, solids are substances that have a definite shape. Unless an outside force causes the shape to change, a solid will stay the same shape. Even a rubber band, which can be stretched, will keep the same shape if it is left alone.

Second, solids have a definite volume. They take up the same amount of room or space. Your desk does not take up more space today than it did yesterday. A book has the same length, width and height all the time, so its volume does not change.

Third, solids have a high density. Because the molecules are packed closely together there is more mass in a given volume in a solid than in a liquid or a gas. Different types of solids have different densities as we saw in lesson 8; however, solids are almost always more dense than liquids and gases. And many items that have low densities, like a ping-pong ball, are actually filled with a gas such as air, making them less dense.

GOD'S DESIGN FOR CHEMISTRY
PROPERTIES OF MATTER

Introduction to Chemistry

Measurement of Matter

States of Matter

Classifications of Matter

Solutions

Food Chemistry

Unit Activity & Conclusion

Solids are formed when a liquid is cooled. Often, if a liquid is cooled slowly the molecules have time to line up in regular patterns and form crystals. If a liquid is cooled quickly, the molecules are frozen in random order so crystals cannot form. Because of this, some solids have different characteristics even if they are made of the same substance. For example, graphite and diamond are both solids comprised of carbon atoms. Yet graphite is a very soft slippery solid, and diamond is the hardest substance on earth. Graphite is formed when carbon atoms cool quickly and diamond is formed when carbon atoms cool very slowly and under great pressure. Similarly, crystallized sulfur is a hard rock-like substance but sulfur that is cooled quickly forms a rubbery substance.

The majority of elements, the pure building blocks that all other substances on earth are made from, are solids. Only two elements, mercury and bromine, are liquids at normal temperatures. Eleven elements are gases and all the other elements are solid at room temperature. So look around and you will find solids everywhere.

TESTING FOR SOLIDS:

In this activity we will dentify which substances are solids and which are not. Gather together a wooden block, a rock, a metal spoon and some honey. For each substance ask the following questions.

1. Does it take up the same amount of room if you put it in another container? (All four objects will take up the same amount of space. This is a characteristic of solids and liquids because they do not expand to fill their containers.)

2. Is it dense, or does it float? (None of these objects floats, so they are all denser than air. Being dense is a characteristic of most solids and liquids.)

3. Does its shape stay the same if I move it or put it in another container? (The honey will not keep its shape, but the others will; therefore, honey cannot be a solid.)

4. Is it a solid? (If you answered yes to all three questions, the object is a solid. Honey is not a solid because it does not keep its shape.)

WHAT DID WE LEARN?

What are three characteristics of solids? (They keep their shape, they have a definite volume, they are denser than most liquids and gases and their molecules are closely packed together.)

How do large crystals form in solids? (If the liquid cools down very slowly, the molecules may be able to line up in regular patterns to make crystals.)

What state is the most common for the basic elements? (Nearly 90% of the elements are solids.)

GOD'S DESIGN FOR CHEMISTRY
PROPERTIES OF MATTER

Introduction to Chemistry

Measurement of Matter

States of Matter

Classifications of Matter

Solutions

Food Chemistry

Unit Activity & Conclusion

TAKING IT FURTHER

Is Silly Putty a solid or a liquid? (Silly Putty may seem like a solid. Yet if you leave it sitting in one place for very long, it will start to flatten out. Because it does not hold its shape it is really a very thick liquid.)

FUN FACT

Over hundreds of years, window glass becomes thicker at the bottom than at the top because the molecules flow downward due to the pull of gravity. Glass is considered a super-cooled liquid and not a solid, because it does not truly keep its shape.

Introduction to Chemistry

Measurement of Matter

States of Matter

Classifications of Matter

Solutions

Food Chemistry

Unit Activity & Conclusion

LESSON 13

LIQUIDS

CAN YOU POUR IT?

SUPPLY LIST:

Water
Vegetable Oil
Honey
Hand lotion
Dish soap
Baking sheet
1 copy of "Viscosity Worksheet" per child (pg. 47)

We have seen that matter can take on one of three different states: solid, liquid or gas. When a substance has enough energy that the molecules can easily slide over one another, but not enough energy to easily move away from one another, it is called a liquid. The molecules are held close to each other, yet they move in a random order. A liquid has more kinetic energy than a solid of the same substance.

Because the molecules in a liquid can move, a liquid does not have a definite shape like a solid does. A liquid will take on the shape of its container. Also, a liquid has a definite volume that can be measured. The molecules are close together so liquids are more dense than gases. Some liquids are more dense than some solids, but in general, liquids are less dense than solids, and gases are much less dense than liquids and solids.

Have you noticed that some liquids are thicker than others? If the molecules have a strong attraction for each other, they do not flow easily. A thick liquid is said to be viscous or to have high viscosity. Viscosity is a measurement of how strongly a substance's molecules are attracted to each other. When we think of liquids we usually think of water. Water is the most common liquid on earth. Water has a relatively low viscosity. It flows easily. You can easily pour it from one container to another. What other liquids can you think of that have a low viscosity? Milk, pop and many other drinks are mostly water and therefore have a low viscosity. Other liquids have a high viscosity as you will see in the following activity.

45

GOD'S DESIGN FOR CHEMISTRY
PROPERTIES OF MATTER

Introduction
to Chemistry

Measurement
of Matter

States of Matter

Classifications
of Matter

Solutions

Food Chemistry

Unit Activity
& Conclusion

OBSERVING VISCOSITY:

Complete the "Viscosity Worksheet."

(Ideas for very thick liquids include hair gel, Silly Putty, hair conditioner or molasses.)

WHAT DID WE LEARN?

Which has more kinetic energy, a solid or a liquid? (A liquid)

What shape does a liquid have? (The shape of its container)

What is viscosity? (A measure of how strongly the liquid's molecules are attracted to each other.)

TAKING IT FURTHER

How is a liquid similar to a solid? (Both a solid and a liquid are much denser than a gas, both have a definite volume that can be measured, the molecules of both are close together.)

How is a liquid different from a solid? (Its molecules move freely over one another and its shape changes when you put it in a different container.)

How would you change a solid into a liquid? (You melt it by adding more energy, usually in the form of heat.)

VISCOSITY WORKSHEET

To understand that some liquids can be thicker than others we need to study several different liquids. For each of the liquids on the chart below, observe the liquid in its original container. Then feel a small amount of each liquid with your fingers and record your observations below.

Liquid	How it looks in the container	How it feels when I touch it
Water		
Vegetable Oil		
Dish Soap		
Hand Lotion		
Honey		

Based on your observations, list the five liquids in the order you think would be from thinnest to thickest:

1. _____ (Thinnest)
2. _____
3. _____
4. _____
5. _____ (Thickest)

Now test your hypothesis by placing a ½ teaspoon of each liquid in drops evenly spaced across the short edge of a baking sheet. Lift the edge of the baking sheet several inches and observe as the liquids flow down the sheet.

List the liquids in order of how fast they reached the bottom of the baking sheet. Some liquids may not reach the bottom. List them according to how far they flowed down the sheet.

1. _____ (Fastest/thinnest)
2. _____
3. _____
4. _____
5. _____ (Slowest/thickest)

Was your hypothesis correct? (Did you list them in the correct order?) _____

Try to find a liquid that is thicker than the thickest liquid you just tested. The thickest liquid I could find was _____.

Introduction to Chemistry

Measurement of Matter

States of Matter

Classifications of Matter

Solutions

Food Chemistry

Unit Activity & Conclusion

LESSON 14

GASES

LIGHTER THAN AIR?

SUPPLY LIST:

2 tennis balls
(Note: place one of the balls in the freezer about 30 minutes before you plan to use it.)

What is the most important gas you can think of? You probably said air or oxygen. If you don't have air to breathe you will quickly die. God designed our atmosphere with just the right amount of oxygen to support all life on the planet. We know that air is made up of gases, but what exactly is a gas?

A substance becomes a gas when it has enough energy that the molecules can freely move away from each other. These molecules have overcome the attractive forces that were holding them close to each other. Because the molecules in a gas do not attract each other, a gas does not have a definite shape. The molecules move randomly to fill whatever container the gas is in. Also, for this reason, the gas does not have a definite volume. Its volume expands to fill its container. Because the gas molecules move randomly, they become evenly distributed within the container.

Because it takes a large amount of energy to overcome the attractive forces of most molecules, gas molecules move at very high speeds. They have very high kinetic energy. Air molecules are usually moving at about 490 meters per second. This is fast enough to cross the United States in about 3 hours! However, the molecules do not move all the way across the United States because they move in a straight line until they hit something. When they hit objects they change their direction. Air molecules experience millions of collisions per second. They collide with other air molecules and they collide with any object in their path. This means that billions of atoms hit each square centimeter of everything on earth each second.

GOD'S DESIGN FOR CHEMISTRY
PROPERTIES OF MATTER

Introduction to Chemistry

Measurement of Matter

States of Matter

Classifications of Matter

Solutions

Food Chemistry

Unit Activity & Conclusion

Inside a container, the air molecules collide with each other and with the inside of the container. If only a few molecules were hitting the inside of the container no one would ever notice it. But because there are billions of molecules inside a container, such as a ball, the constant collisions against the inside of the ball create pressure on the inside of the ball. This is called gas pressure. Fortunately, there is gas on the outside of the ball that is also pushing against the ball. This is called atmospheric pressure. At sea level, the amount of pressure applied by the air to one square centimeter is called one atmosphere. As you go up in altitude the air molecules are further apart so there are less molecules and the atmospheric pressure is less.

Even though the air all around us is constantly pressing against our bodies we do not notice it. God designed our bodies perfectly for our environment. Our bodies naturally exert an outward pressure equal to about 1 atmosphere. Our bodies are also designed to adjust to changes in atmospheric pressure. Have you ever gone up in the mountains or on an airplane and had your ears "pop?" That was your body adjusting to a change in pressure. God created the air we need to breathe and designed our bodies to adapt to the air pressure.

OBSERVING AIR PRESSURE:

Why does a ball bounce? (It is because the air molecules inside the ball are pressing against the inside of the ball. So when a ball hits the floor, the molecules inside it push back against the floor, causing the ball to bounce up.)

Do gas molecules move faster when they are warm or when they are cold? (The warmer the molecules are, the faster they will be moving.)

With this knowledge, make a guess as to which ball will bounce higher, a warm tennis ball or a cold tennis ball.

Take a tennis ball at room temperature and a tennis ball that has been in the freezer for at least 30 minutes and drop them together from the same height onto the floor. Which ball bounced highest? (The warm ball will bounce higher.)

Why does the warmer ball bounce higher? (The molecules inside the ball are moving faster so more particles collide with the inside of the ball when it hits the floor. This gives the warm ball more energy to bounce back than the cold ball has.)

WHAT DID WE LEARN?

When is a substance called a gas? (When it has enough energy for the molecules to break apart from each other and move freely.)

What is the shape of a gas? (It is the shape of its container.)

In which state of matter are the molecules moving the fastest? (In a gas)

What is atmospheric pressure? (The pressure applied to a surface by the collision of the air molecules with that surface.)

GOD'S DESIGN FOR CHEMISTRY
PROPERTIES OF MATTER

Introduction to Chemistry

Measurement of Matter

States of Matter

Classifications of Matter

Solutions

Food Chemistry

Unit Activity & Conclusion

TAKING IT FURTHER

How is a gas similar to a liquid? (The molecules of both a gas and a liquid can move around and they both take on the shape of their containers.)

How is a gas different from a liquid? (Gas molecules have much more energy, they freely move away from each other, and they collide with other molecules and objects billions of times a second. Gas expands to fill its container so it does not have a definite volume.)

Why is it necessary that a space suit be pressurized in outer space? (God designed our bodies to operate in an environment where there is pressure on our bodies. If this pressure were not there, we would die. Since there is no air in space there is no air pressure, so space suits must provide the pressure necessary for the astronauts.)

Introduction to Chemistry

Measurement of Matter

States of Matter

Classifications of Matter

Solutions

Food Chemistry

Unit Activity & Conclusion

GAS LAWS

RULES TO LIVE BY

SUPPLY LIST:

Empty 1 gallon milk carton   Balloon
Microwave oven
Cloth tape measure or string and a ruler

Understanding how matter behaves under different conditions has always been a goal of scientists. Many scientists make observations and conduct experiments to try to predict what will happen under various conditions. They cool materials down or heat them up to see how they react. They put them under pressure and see what happens. They combine different substances together to try to make new materials. All of these experiments have shown us important properties and have led to many important discoveries. Two of the most important discoveries related to gases are called gas laws because they describe how all gases behave, no matter what the gas is made of.

The first gas law was discovered in 1660 by a scientist named Robert Boyle, and is called Boyle's Law. Boyle discovered that as pressure on a gas increases, the volume of the gas decreases. Conversely, as the pressure goes down, the volume of the gas goes up. He also discovered that this relationship is proportional. That means that if the pressure is cut in half the volume doubles and if the pressure is 3 times what is was initially, the volume will be 1/3 of its original volume. This relationship between the volume of a gas and the pressure is true for all gases, as long as the temperature of the gas does not change.

The temperature of a gas can affect its volume as well. This relationship was studied about 100 years later by a scientist named Jacque Charles and is called Charles' Law. Charles discovered that the higher the temperature, the greater the volume of the gas. If the temperature of the gas doubles, the

GOD'S DESIGN FOR CHEMISTRY
PROPERTIES OF MATTER

Introduction to Chemistry

Measurement of Matter

States of Matter

Classifications of Matter

Solutions

Food Chemistry

Unit Activity & Conclusion

volume of the gas will double as well. You saw the effect of this relationship in the last lesson when you tested how high a cold ball would bounce. As the temperature of the gas decreases the molecules have less energy so they do not move around as much and will not take up as much room. This is true only if the pressure on the gas remains the same.

So you see that pressure and temperature both affect the volume of a gas. The gas laws say that if temperature does not change, the volume goes up as the pressure goes down; and if the pressure does not change, the volume goes up as the temperature goes up.

HOT AND COLD GAS:

It is somewhat difficult to test the effects of changing pressure on gas at home because changing the pressure requires a vacuum chamber. However, it is very easy to change the temperature of the gas while keeping the pressure the same and see the change in volume. You can test this two different ways.

First, fill a balloon with air and tie the end of the balloon. Next, measure the circumference of the balloon. Place the balloon in the freezer for 15 minutes. Remove the cold balloon from the freezer and measure its circumference. The circumference of the balloon should be smaller because the air molecules are cooler and therefore take up less room inside the balloon.

For a more dramatic example do the following. Fill a sink half full with cold water. Place a ½ cup of water inside an empty plastic gallon milk carton. Do not place the cap on the carton. Place the carton in a microwave oven and heat for 30 seconds. Use hot pads or oven mitts to remove the carton from the microwave oven. Immediately place the cap on the carton and set the carton in the sink of cold water. As the gas cools down it will have less volume and the milk carton will "shrink" before your eyes.

WHAT DID WE LEARN?

If temperature remains constant, what happens to the volume of a gas when the pressure is increased? (The volume is decreased.)

If pressure remains constant, what happens to the volume of a gas when the temperature is increased? (The volume increases.)

What are two different ways to increase the volume of a gas? (Decrease the pressure or increase the temperature.)

TAKING IT FURTHER

Why might you need to check the air in your bike tires before you go for a ride on a cold day? (The volume of air may be decreased enough by the cold temperatures that you may need to add some air so your tires will not be flat.)

Why do you think increasing pressure decreases the volume of a gas?

(The pressure forces the molecules closer together so they take up less space.)

Why do you think increasing temperature increases the volume of a gas? (The increase in the temperature adds energy to the molecules causing them to move faster so they spread out more and take up more space.)

What might happen to the volume of a gas when the pressure is increased and the temperature is increased at the same time? (It depends on how much the pressure and temperature are increased. It is possible that the volume could remain the same. It could also increase or decrease. Because you are changing two things at once, you can't be certain of the effect.)

FUN FACT

Weather balloons are very large helium-filled balloons that are used to carry weather instruments up through the atmosphere to measure such things as temperature, pressure and wind at high altitudes. When a weather balloon is released, it is only partially inflated. This is because as the balloon rises the pressure drops and the volume of gas expands inside the balloon. If the balloon were fully inflated before it was released, it would explode at a lower altitude and the weatherman would not get the needed data.

GOD'S DESIGN FOR CHEMISTRY
PROPERTIES OF MATTER

Introduction to Chemistry

Measurement of Matter

States of Matter

Classifications of Matter

Solutions

Food Chemistry

Unit Activity & Conclusion

ROBERT BOYLE

(1627-1691)

Do you have fourteen brothers and sisters? Robert Boyle, a very famous chemist, did. Robert was the fourteenth of fifteen children in his family. He was born in Munster, Ireland in 1627. Robert's father was the Earl of Cork and he was not only blessed with many children, but he was considered the wealthiest man in all of Great Britain.

The Boyle family had a deep faith in God and Robert learned to spend time every day reading his Bible. He was a devout Christian. In fact, throughout his life, Boyle was offered many important positions of leadership in the Anglican Church. However, he refused, believing that God had called him to other areas of ministry.

The most important area of ministry that Boyle had was the pursuit of biblical science. When Boyle began his scientific studies, chemistry as we know it did not exist. Instead, the study was called alchemy and it was a strange mix of science and mysticism. Robert Boyle, however, believed that there were definite scientific properties to elements that did not need mystical explanations. With this in mind, he performed many experiments. He was the first to define an element as a substance that cannot be broken down by ordinary chemical means. Boyle recognized numerous elements when many other people only recognized four types of matter. Boyle was also the first scientist to distinguish between mixtures and compounds. In fact, Boyle has been described as the leading chemist of the 17th century.

Boyle viewed his work in science as his ministry and God blessed his work. In many lectures, Boyle taught that Christianity could be defended intellectually and was more reasonable to believe than other philosophies of the day.

In addition to his scientific work, Robert Boyle was also a great supporter of world missions. He used his own wealth to support missionaries to Ireland, Scotland, Wales, India and North America. He also paid to have the gospels and the Book of Acts translated into Turkish, Arabic and Malayan, and to have the entire Bible translated into Irish.

Robert Boyle is best remembered for his gas laws and other contributions to chemistry; however, Christians should also remember him for his service to God in defending Christianity to the scientific world of his day, and for his work in spreading the gospel around the world.

States of Matter Quiz
Lessons 10-15

Use a word or phrase from the list below to fill in the blanks.

Adding heat   Solid   Removing heat   Liquid   Gas

1. The three states of matter are _____, _____, and _____.

2. _____ causes the molecules in matter to move more quickly.

3. _____ causes the molecules in matter to move more slowly.

4. _____ is required to change a gas into a liquid.

5. _____ is required to change a solid into a liquid.

Write S beside the statement if it describes a property of a solid, L if it describes a liquid, and G if it describes a gas. Some statements describe more than one state of matter.

6. _____ Molecules are close together.

7. _____ Molecules are far apart.

8. _____ It takes on the shape of its container.

9. _____ Molecules move very quickly.

10. _____ Molecules slide over each other.

11. _____ Easily compressed.

12. _____ Has a defined shape.

13. _____ Has a defined volume.

14. _____ Molecules only vibrate.

15. _____ Not easily compressed.

Answer True or False for each statement below.

16. _____ Thick liquids have a high viscosity.

17. _____ As the temperature of a gas increases, its volume decreases.

18. _____ As the pressure of a gas increases, its volume decreases.

19. _____ A ball will usually bounce better on a warm day than on a cold one.

20. _____ Molecules in a viscous liquid are not strongly attracted to each other.

21. _____ There is a direct relationship between the temperature of a gas and its volume.

22. _____ Crystals are more likely to form when a solid cools slowly.

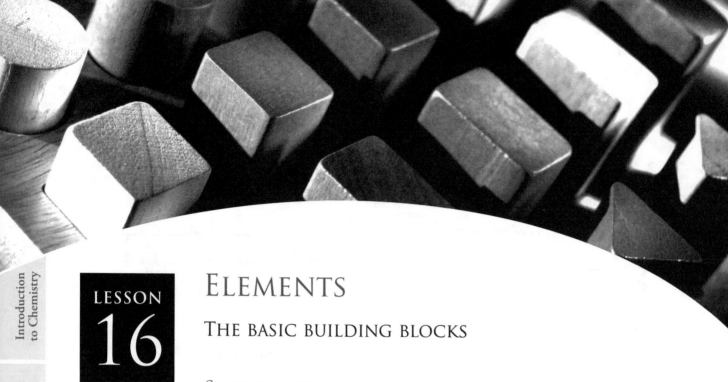

Introduction to Chemistry

Measurement of Matter

States of Matter

Classifications of Matter

Solutions

Food Chemistry

Unit Activity & Conclusion

LESSON 16

ELEMENTS

THE BASIC BUILDING BLOCKS

SUPPLY LIST:

Jigsaw puzzle

In order to understand any complex subject, it is necessary to break it into smaller pieces. One way to do this is by classification. Classification is grouping things together according to their similar characteristics. For example, most living things are classified as either plants or animals. Animals are then classified as either vertebrates or invertebrates, depending on whether or not they have a backbone.

In a similar way, scientists have classified all matter by analyzing what it is made of and then grouping similar types of matter together. Matter is classified into three groups: elements, compounds and mixtures. An element is defined as a substance that cannot be broken down into simpler substances by ordinary chemical means. Elements are the simplest kinds of matter. Some common elements that you are familiar with are oxygen, helium, gold, silver and carbon. Compounds are substances that are formed when two or more elements combine chemically to make a new substance. Common compounds include water, which is a combination of oxygen and hydrogen, and carbon dioxide, which is a combination of oxygen and carbon. A mixture is formed when two or more substances are mixed together but do not chemically combine to form a different substance. Common mixtures include milk and salt water. Both elements and compounds are considered pure substances, but mixtures are not pure because they contain more than one kind of substance.

There are 92 elements that occur naturally and more than 20 additional elements that have been made by man. Elements consist of basic building blocks called atoms. An atom is the smallest unit of an element that has the properties of that element. All substances on earth are made from some

GOD'S DESIGN FOR CHEMISTRY
PROPERTIES OF MATTER

Introduction to Chemistry

Measurement of Matter

States of Matter

Classifications of Matter

Solutions

Food Chemistry

Unit Activity & Conclusion

combination of the elements. However, although everything is made from elements, elements rarely occur by themselves as single atoms in nature. Most atoms join with other atoms, either of the same kind or different kinds, to form molecules. For example, the air we breathe is mostly nitrogen and oxygen. However, it is very unlikely to find a single nitrogen atom or a single oxygen atom. Most nitrogen and oxygen atoms combine in pairs (called diatomic molecules). Each molecule is made of two nitrogen or two oxygen atoms connected together.

Each element has a unique symbol derived from its name. The symbol is usually the first letter of the name followed by another letter; however, some elements are denoted simply by the first letters of their names. Some symbols include O for oxygen, H for hydrogen, He for helium, and Si for silicon. A few symbols come from the Latin name for the element. For example Ag is the symbol for silver whose Latin name is *argentum* and Fe is the symbol for iron whose Latin name is *ferrum*.

Metal names often end in "um" or "ium" and non-metals usually end in "n" or "ine". Many man-made elements are named for people or places such as Einsteinium or Californium. Recently discovered elements are called by their electron structures: pentium, herium, ununbium, ununtrium, etc. until they are given official names.

We are very familiar with many of the elements around us. Nearly everyone knows what gold, silver, aluminum, oxygen, carbon, hydrogen and helium are. These familiar building blocks are used to form every other substance around us. As we learn about each element, we can thank God for His wonderful design of each substance.

CLASSIFICATION EXERCISE:

When scientists first started trying to figure out what things were made of they had a difficult task. The ancient Greeks believed that everything was made of either fire, air, earth or water. Today, we know that things are much more complex than just four elements. To appreciate the process of classification, dump the pieces of a jigsaw puzzle in the middle of the table. This mixed up pile represents what early scientists understood about the basic building blocks of matter.

As scientists began to learn more about matter, they discovered that some types of matter had similar characteristics. With the puzzle, you can sort pieces by their shape. Put all of the edge pieces in one pile and all of the inside pieces in another pile. This is similar to how scientists began to group matter with similar characteristics together.

Now sort the edge pieces into piles by their similar shapes. Some pieces may have an indent on each side, some may have no indents at all.

Introduction to Chemistry

Measurement of Matter

States of Matter

Classifications of Matter

Solutions

Food Chemistry

Unit Activity & Conclusion

Next, sort the interior pieces by similar shapes such as the ones shown below. Your puzzle pieces may be shaped differently. Find common shapes and sort the pieces according to the common shapes. This is how scientists began classifying matter—by looking at what was the same and what was different.

Once you have the pieces sorted, with each shape representing an element, see if you can make a small picture with a few of the pieces from the different piles. This is like making a compound. A few elements put together in a certain way make a new substance, just as a few pieces put together in a certain way make a new shape or picture.

When you put the whole puzzle together, it is just like when God put all of the elements together and created the beautiful world we live in.

WHAT DID WE LEARN?

What is an element? (It is a substance that cannot be broken down by ordinary chemical means—an atom.)

What is a compound? (It is a substance that is formed when two or more elements combine chemically—a molecule.)

What is a mixture? (It is a combination of two or more substances that do not make a new substance.)

TAKING IT FURTHER

If a new element was discovered and it was named newmaterialium, would you expect it to be a metal or a non-metal? (It would probably be a metal because most metal names end in "um" or "ium.")

Is salt an element, a compound or a mixture? (Salt is a compound made from sodium and chlorine. It can be broken apart into its elements. But when they are put together they form a new substance.)

Is soda pop an element, compound or mixture? (It is a mixture of water, sugar, flavorings and other substances, but it is not a new substance.)

WILLIAM PROUT

(1785-1850)

A doctor, a chemist and a father of seven, William Prout was a meticulous man who was born on January 15, 1785, in the town of Horton, in Gloucestershire, England. He was the oldest of three brothers born to a tenant farmer named John Prout. Even though he was not physically strong, he left school at the age of thirteen to work on his father's farm.

He was aware of his lack of education, so when he was seventeen he left home to change this. He went to a school in Wiltshire to learn Latin and Greek. Three years later he entered a classical seminary in Redland to further his studies. To cover the costs of his schooling, he taught the younger students. This is when he became interested in chemistry. Because of this interest, he was encouraged to study medicine, which he did at Edinburgh University. He graduated in 1811 with his M.D.

William moved to London to complete his studies and become a licensed physician. In 1813 he set up a medical practice. At that time he also married Agnes Adam, oldest daughter of Dr. Alexander Adam. They had seven children together.

In addition to practicing medicine, Prout began to study chemistry in many forms. Using the test results from other chemists relating to the atomic weights of different elements, he suggested that all other elements were whole number multiples of the atomic weight of hydrogen. This suggestion was highly controversial. It changed the notion of the indivisible atom. His suggestion was rejected by some of the top chemists of his day; however, other experiments throughout the 19th century eventually proved this to be true. In one of his experiments, he showed that one volume of oxygen and two volumes of hydrogen would form two volumes of steam. From this he stated that water was made up of two hydrogen atoms and one oxygen atom. Today this seems obvious, but in the early 19th century this was astounding.

He later turned his attentions to developing new techniques for studying organic chemistry. Sparing no expense in his search for more accuracy, he developed many of his own instruments, including his own equipment to remove moisture from chemicals. He performed a multitude of experiments, but he was only willing to publish a few of his results as he did not want to put any information out until he was sure his measurements were completely accurate. Because of his work and drive for accuracy, by 1827 he had become the leading physiological chemist in England.

Prout devoted much of his research to understanding the chemicals in the bodies of animals and humans. His work included developing new methods for studying and separating compounds. He often used himself as the test subject. For example, he measured the carbon dioxide in his breath at different times of the day and night, before and after eating, and in various emotional and physical states.

In addition to studying the chemicals in his breath, Prout also worked to find the properties and origins of blood. Based on his study of blood and the respiratory system, he suggested that blood flowed through the lung to remove carbon, in the form of carbon dioxide, from the system. He also studied the components that make up urine in animals and men. He found that the differences between healthy and diseased urine could be readily explained and understood.

He studied animal digestive systems to see the chemical changes that took place. He examined the contents of rabbits' stomachs at various times after they had eaten and found that acids where introduced into the system at certain locations. This led to the discovery that the acid found in the stomach is hydrochloric acid. He also felt certain that the respiration and the assimilation of food and the production of heat in animals were all linked in the maintenance of life for warm-blooded animals; he just was not sure of the mechanisms that linked them. William also felt that the foods a person eats could have an effect on the person's mental abilities.

Prout made great strides in understanding chemicals and especially in understanding their effects on human and animal bodies. However, he did not live to see the results of many of his discoveries. In his youth he had suffered many intense earaches and in the 1830s he became deaf. At this time he withdrew from the scientific society. He died in 1850.

Introduction to Chemistry

Measurement of Matter

States of Matter

Classifications of Matter

Solutions

Food Chemistry

Unit Activity & Conclusion

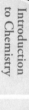

COMPOUNDS

MAKING NEW SUBSTANCES

LESSON 17

SUPPLY LIST:

2 small jars (small baby food jars or test tubes)
Copper wire (at least 3 feet)
6 volt battery (big square battery)
Baking soda

Everything around us is made up of atoms. These atoms sometimes occur by themselves, but usually they combine with other atoms to form new kinds of matter. When atoms combine together they form molecules. If two atoms of the same type of element combine they form what is called a diatomic molecule, but if two or more different types of elements combine to form a molecule it is called a compound. The most familiar compound is water. Water is formed when two hydrogen atoms and one oxygen atom combine.

When atoms of different elements combine to form a new substance, the new substance usually has completely different characteristics from those of the original atoms. For example, hydrogen and oxygen are both gases at room temperature, but when they combine to form water, they become a substance that is usually a liquid at room temperature. Similarly, sodium is a soft metal and chlorine is a poisonous gas, but when they combine chemically they form a solid that you eat every day—table salt.

There are more than 110 known elements and they can be combined in innumerable ways. Scientists have identified over three million different compounds. A few of the very familiar compounds include salt, sugar, water, starch, alcohol, carbon dioxide and chlorophyll.

Some elements are very reactive and combine easily with other elements. Others are very stable and do not combine easily with any other substance. Hydrogen is very reactive, but nitrogen is very stable. God

Introduction to Chemistry

Measurement of Matter

States of Matter

Classifications of Matter

Solutions

Food Chemistry

Unit Activity & Conclusion

designed the earth's atmosphere to have a large percentage of nitrogen specifically because it does not easily react with other substances. If the atmosphere was 100 % oxygen, fires would burn out of control, but the nitrogen in the atmosphere dilutes the oxygen and keeps life on earth safe. You can learn more about why some elements are more reactive than others in *God's Design for Chemistry—Properties of Atoms and Molecules.*

Scientists use symbols called chemical formulas to describe what a compound is made of. The symbol for each kind of atom is followed by a subscript number showing how many of that type of atom are in the molecule. Water has two hydrogen atoms and one oxygen atom so its chemical formula is H_2O. Sugar (sucrose) has 12 carbon atoms, 22 hydrogen atoms and 11 oxygen atoms so its chemical formula is $C_{12}H_{22}O_{11}$. All other compounds have similar chemical formulas. Some are simple, others are very complex.

The number of each kind of atom and how they are connected together determines what substance is formed. Sugar and alcohol are both made from only carbon, hydrogen and oxygen atoms, but they are very different substances because the number of each kind of atom in the molecules is different. Alcohol is very different from sugar because it has only 4 carbon atoms, 8 hydrogen atoms, and 1 oxygen atom (C_4H_8O), whereas sugar has 12 carbon, 22 hydrogen and 11 oxygen atoms. God designed atoms so they can be combined in an astounding variety of ways so that we can experience this amazing world around us.

ELECTROLYSIS OF WATER:

A water molecule is made when two hydrogen atoms bond with an oxygen atom. The bond between these atoms is fairly strong but can be broken by an electrical charge. As the electrons flow through the water, the molecules break apart and the hydrogen and oxygen return to their gas form. To observe this process you can do the following experiment.

Fill a sink with water and place two small jars in the water so they are completely filled with water. Cut two pieces of copper wire long enough to reach from a battery on the counter into the jars. Strip off an inch of insulation from the ends of each wire. Attach one end of a wire to the positive terminal and one end of the other wire to the negative terminal of the battery.

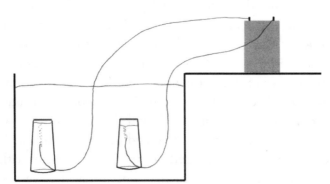

Place the end of one wire in one jar and the other wire in the second jar.

Hold the jars inverted in the water so that the mouth of each jar is below the surface of the water and

GOD'S DESIGN FOR CHEMISTRY
PROPERTIES OF MATTER

Introduction
to Chemistry

Measurement
of Matter

States of Matter

Classifications
of Matter

Solutions

Food Chemistry

Unit Activity
& Conclusion

the jar remains filled with water. Sprinkle a teaspoon of baking soda in the water and stir to help it dissolve. The baking soda helps encourage the electricity to flow through the water.

After a short time you should notice bubbles forming on the ends of each of the wires. These bubbles will slowly push the water out of the jars. After a few minutes it should become obvious that one jar is being filled with gas faster than the other jar. Answer the following questions.

1. What do you think is in each jar? (They may suggest air. The correct answer is hydrogen in one jar and oxygen in the other.)

2. Which jar do you think has the hydrogen in it? (The jar that has more gas has the hydrogen. Remember, there are 2 hydrogen atoms for every oxygen atom in the water.)

3. Why do you think the battery is needed to separate the atoms? (Energy is required to break the bonds of the molecule and the battery supplies electrical energy.)

WHAT DID WE LEARN?

What is a compound? (A substance that is formed when two or more different kinds of atoms are chemically joined together.)

What is the smallest bit of an element? (An atom)

What is the smallest bit of a compound? (A molecule)

Do compounds behave the same way as the atoms that they are made from? (Not usually. Oxygen gas and hydrogen gas act very differently than liquid water or water vapor.)

TAKING IT FURTHER

The symbol for carbon dioxide is CO_2. What atoms combine to form this molecule? (One carbon atom and two oxygen atoms.)

The air consists of nitrogen and oxygen molecules. Is air a compound? Why or why not? (The air is not a compound because the nitrogen and oxygen molecules do not bond with each other to form a different substance. Instead, air is a mixture of gases.)

Introduction to Chemistry

Measurement of Matter

States of Matter

Classifications of Matter

Solutions

Food Chemistry

Unit Activity & Conclusion

WATER

GOD'S COMPOUND FOR LIFE

SUPPLY LIST:

1 copy of "Water, Water Everywhere" for each child (pg. 67)

Over 70% of the surface of the earth is covered with water. This fact, more than any other, is why life is able to exist on earth and not on any other planet in our solar system. God designed water to be the perfect compound to sustain life.

Water is nearly a universal solvent. This means that it dissolves nearly everything it touches. Obviously, some things dissolve more easily than others, but it is very difficult to obtain completely pure water because water even dissolves very tiny amounts of glass or metal from its container. This is a very important quality of water that most other liquids do not possess. Because so many substances dissolve in water, it is used to transport nutrients throughout plants. And because blood is comprised of mostly water, it can transport all the chemicals you need throughout your body.

One reason that water is such a good solvent is its unique shape. The hydrogen atoms attach to the oxygen atom at a 105° angle giving the molecule a lopsided shape. This means that the hydrogen side of the molecule is slightly positive and the oxygen side is slightly negative, which allows the water to break apart most other substances and hold the atoms away from each other. This process will be explained more in later lessons.

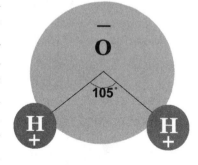

Water has no flavor or smell, but it is in nearly everything we eat or drink. It is found throughout all plants and animals. Water is necessary for nearly every bodily function. This is why it is so important to drink enough

Introduction
to Chemistry

Measurement
of Matter

States of Matter

Classifications
of Matter

Solutions

Food Chemistry

Unit Activity
& Conclusion

water every day.

Besides being necessary for life, water is very useful in many natural and man-made processes. Water is one of the main ingredients needed for photosynthesis. In photosynthesis, plants use water and carbon dioxide to produce sugar. Water is important in farming to produce the food our world needs. Water is also a key ingredient in many manufacturing processes. Water is necessary for the production of paper, electronic circuits, food, beverages and many other manufactured goods.

Water is also used for recreation. Water sports are some of the most popular activities. Also, water is used for decoration. Fountains and waterfalls are a common sight in many areas. In addition, water is needed for many daily activities such as bathing, laundry, cooking and gardening.

With so many uses for water you might be concerned that the world will run out of water. However, as you learned in lesson 6, God designed the world so that water is constantly recycled. Even though plants and animals use water in their normal growing processes, they also release water back into the atmosphere. Also, when a plant or animal dies, the water in its body is released. Water is also a by-product of many chemical reactions. For example, when the space shuttle takes off it uses liquid hydrogen and liquid oxygen for fuel. The unused molecules combine to form large clouds of steam that billow from the shuttle as it takes off. Also, many new cars are now using hydrogen as fuel and they produce water as the end product instead of carbon monoxide. So water is continually being added to the earth at about the same rate it is being used.

The next time you watch the rain or drink a glass of water, thank God for creating water so life could exist on earth.

HUNTING FOR WATER:

Using a copy of the "Water, Water Everywhere" worksheet, record all of the uses of water in your home for the past day. After filling out the worksheet, see if you forgot any of the following uses:

Food, water, beverages, washing dishes, cooking, making ice, growing house plants, water for pets, brushing teeth, toilets, bath/shower, washing hands/face, wiping counters, washing windows, laundry, mopping floors, watering grass, breathing, sweating/cooling your body, digestion, blood circulation, blinking, elimination of wastes, making of new cells, etc.

These are just a few ideas. What ideas do you have that are not on this list?

WHAT DID WE LEARN?

What two kinds of atoms combine to form water? (Hydrogen and oxygen)

Why is water called a universal solvent? (Because a large variety of substances can be dissolved in water.)

What is unique about the water molecule that makes it able to dissolve

GOD'S DESIGN FOR CHEMISTRY
PROPERTIES OF MATTER

Introduction
to Chemistry

Measurement
of Matter

States of Matter

Classifications
of Matter

Solutions

Food Chemistry

Unit Activity
& Conclusion

so many substances? (The hydrogen atoms attach to the oxygen atom at a 105° angle, causing the charge to be unevenly distributed.)

TAKING IT FURTHER

What would happen to your body if oxygen could not be dissolved in water? (Your blood would not be able to take oxygen to the cells in your body and you would die.)

Why is it important for mothers with nursing babies to drink lots of water? (Water is used in the production of milk.)

FUN FACT

Excess water is released from plant leaves through tiny holes on the bottom of the leaves, called stomata. This process is called transpiration.

WATER, WATER EVERYWHERE

Water is a vital part of life. God created water to keep plants and animals alive on earth. Because it is so important, we use water in many ways every day. See how many ways you can find water being used in your home. Fill in the chart below with every way you and your family have used water in your home in the past day.

Location	Ways water is used in this part of the home
Kitchen	
Living room	
Bathroom	
Laundry room	
Yard	
Anywhere else you happen to be (Ways your body uses water)	

Introduction to Chemistry

Measurement of Matter

States of Matter

Classifications of Matter

Solutions

Food Chemistry

Unit Activity & Conclusion

LESSON 19

MIXTURES

ALL MIXED UP

SUPPLY LIST:

Coffee filter
Funnel

Orange juice
Cup

Elements and compounds are pure substances. They each consist of only one kind of material. Yet most things in the universe are not pure substances. Most items are a combination of two or more elements or compounds mixed together. These substances are called mixtures.

All mixtures have the following characteristics.

1. Mixtures are comprised of two or more pure substances.

2. Each substance keeps its own properties and does not create a new substance.

3. The different substances can be separated by physical means. This means that the different substances can be separated by filtering, boiling, sorting or some other non-chemical method.

4. The substances in a mixture can be found in any proportion. In a compound such as carbon dioxide, the ratio of atoms is always the same; there are always 2 oxygen atoms to each carbon atom. But in a mixture such as salt water there could be 1 part water to 1 part salt or 100 parts water to 1 part salt or any other proportion, and it would still be salt water.

One of the most abundant mixtures on earth is seawater. Seawater consists of water, salt and a variety of other minerals, as well as tiny bits of sand, plants and other materials. Each of these substances has its own physical properties such as boiling point, density, hardness, etc. And each item can be separated from the water if the water is boiled away. If you add

GOD'S DESIGN FOR CHEMISTRY
PROPERTIES OF MATTER

Introduction to Chemistry

Measurement of Matter

States of Matter

Classifications of Matter

Solutions

Food Chemistry

Unit Activity & Conclusion

more salt to seawater it is still seawater. And if you filter out the sand and other debris, you still have seawater. Other common mixtures include air (which is a mixture of gases), milk (which is a mixture of liquids and solids) and stainless steel (which is a mixture of iron, carbon and chromium).

Mixtures can be classified by how the materials are distributed throughout it. If the substances in the mixture are evenly distributed it is called a homogeneous mixture. Air and seawater are homogeneous mixtures. A mixture in which the substances are not evenly distributed is called a heterogeneous mixture. Granite is an example of a heterogeneous mixture. Granite is made from a combination of the minerals feldspar, quartz and mica. These minerals can be found in any proportion and are not evenly mixed. One piece of granite may be mostly feldspar and another may have a large chunk of quartz with bits of mica spread around in it.

Although pure substances, such as elements like oxygen and compounds like water, are vitally important, most things around you are a combination of elements and compounds mixed together and are thus mixtures.

SEPARATING A MIXTURE:

To see how a mixture is different from a compound, do the following.

Line a funnel with a coffee filter. Place the funnel so the contents will drip into a cup or bottle. Shake up a container of orange juice, then slowly pour some orange juice through the filter. Reserve some orange juice for the end of the experiment. The water will flow through the filter and the orange pulp will be trapped in the filter. This may take several hours depending on the filter you use. Do not squeeze the filter. After most of the liquid has passed through the filter, compare the liquid to some of the original orange juice. The liquid should be much clearer. Some of the orange pulp may be small enough to pass through the filter, but much of it will be trapped by the filter.

Orange juice is a mixture of orange pulp and water. The water is still water no matter how much orange pulp is mixed in with it. The orange pulp is still orange pulp even when it is mixed into the water. So orange juice is not a new substance, just a mixture of substances.

WHAT DID WE LEARN?

What are two differences between a compound and a mixture? (A compound is formed when two or more elements combine to form a new substance. A mixture is formed when two or more elements or compounds are combined but do not form a new substance. The elements in a compound are always in the same proportion. The elements or compounds in a mixture can be in any proportion.)

What is a homogeneous mixture? (One in which all of the substances are evenly distributed.)

What is a heterogeneous mixture? (One in which all of the substances are not evenly distributed.)

GOD'S DESIGN FOR CHEMISTRY
PROPERTIES OF MATTER

Introduction to Chemistry

Measurement of Matter

States of Matter

Classifications of Matter

Solutions

Food Chemistry

Unit Activity & Conclusion

Name three common mixtures. (Possible answers include air, milk, granite, orange juice and seawater.)

Taking it further

If a soft metal is combined with a gas to form a hard solid that doesn't look or act like either of the original substances, is the resulting substance a mixture or a compound? (The result is a compound because the new substance has different characteristics from the original substances. In a mixture, the substances retain their original properties.)

How might you separate the salt from the sand and water in a sample of seawater? (First, you could filter out the sand. Then you could let the water evaporate into the air and the salt would be left behind. This is similar to the experiment you did in lesson 6.)

Introduction to Chemistry

Measurement of Matter

States of Matter

Classifications of Matter

Solutions

Food Chemistry

Unit Activity & Conclusion

LESSON 20

MILK AND CREAM

UDDERLY DELICIOUS

SUPPLY LIST:

2 cups liquid whipping cream   Jar with lid
Sugar   Vanilla extract
Canned spray whipping cream (made with real cream)

One of the most common mixtures found inside refrigerators around the world is milk. In some parts of the world people drink goat's milk; in other parts of the world people drink cow's milk. Cow's milk is a mixture that is approximately 87% water, 5% lactose (a type of sugar), 4% fat, 3% protein and 1% ash. The protein, vitamins and minerals in milk, make this a popular drink and a popular ingredient in many foods.

At one time, milk had to be consumed shortly after it came from the cow because it quickly spoiled. But after a scientist named Louis Pasteur discovered that bacteria were the cause of most food spoilage, and with the invention of the modern refrigerator, milk can now be stored for many days before going bad.

After the cow is milked, the milk undergoes several processes before it reaches the supermarket shelves. The first process is called *pasteurization*, named for Luis Pasteur. In this process the milk is heated to 145 °F for 30 minutes, or to 161 °F for 15 minutes, to kill the bacteria. It is then cooled and stored at temperatures below 45 °F. Most milk that is packaged for drinking experiences a second process called *homogenization*. This process breaks up the fat molecules into tiny bundles so they stay suspended in the liquid of the milk instead of floating to the top.

Some milk, however, is not homogenized. If the milk is not homogenized, the cream, the part containing the fat molecules, will rise to the top of the milk. In the past, people would skim the cream off the top of the milk and use it to make butter, cheese and other products. Today, instead

GOD'S DESIGN FOR CHEMISTRY
PROPERTIES OF MATTER

Introduction
to Chemistry

Measurement
of Matter

States of Matter

Classifications
of Matter

Solutions

Food Chemistry

Unit Activity
& Conclusion

of just letting the cream rise to the top of the vat, the milk is placed in a machine called a separator, which spins the milk and separates the cream from the milk. The cream is then used to make many products including butter, cheese, ice cream and whipped cream. The milk that remains is then sold as skim milk.

Butter is one product that is made from cream. Butter is made by churning or vigorously shaking the cream. This churning causes the fat molecules to combine together to form large clumps. These clumps are then removed and sometimes a small amount of salt and coloring are added before the butter is formed into cubes and packaged to be sold. The liquid left over from the butter making process is called buttermilk. Buttermilk is sold separately and is also used in many products such as pancakes or biscuits.

Another popular product made from cream is whipped cream. Whipped cream is a foam. A foam is a liquid with air trapped inside it. Have you ever seen sea foam? The movement of the waves against the shore causes air bubbles to become trapped between the water molecules. Similarly, if cream is whipped, air molecules become trapped in between the fat molecules, causing the cream to be very fluffy. Usually sugar and vanilla are added to improve the flavor of the whipped cream and make it a delightful topping to any sweet treat.

Finally, one of the most popular cream products is ice cream. Ice cream is a mixture of cream, milk, sugar and other flavors that are frozen into a smooth delicious dessert.

HOW STRONG IS YOUR WHIPPED CREAM?:

The ability of the cream molecules to trap air is called its structural integrity. Let's do an experiment to see which kind of cream has more structural integrity. First, make homemade whipped cream by whipping one cup of cream with an electric mixer on high speed until peaks form. Then gently stir in 1 tablespoon of sugar and 1 teaspoon of vanilla extract. Place a large spoonful of this whipped cream on a plate. Next to this, spray an equal amount of canned spray whipped cream. Be sure the canned whipped cream is made from real cream. Many of the products sold are made from other substances such as vegetable or soybean oil.

Place the plate in the refrigerator for one hour. Check to see which sample looks the most like whipped cream after one hour. Eventually the cream molecules will lose their ability to keep the air molecules trapped. When the air starts to escape, the cream begins to "weep" and becomes runny. Which type of cream would be best to use if you want to make a dessert ahead of time and store it until your dinner guests have finished their dinner?

MAKING BUTTER:

While you are waiting for your whipped cream to break down, you can make some butter. Place one cup of cream in a clean jar and screw the

Introduction
to Chemistry

Measurement
of Matter

States of Matter

Classifications
of Matter

Solutions

Food Chemistry

Unit Activity
& Conclusion

lid on tightly. Shake the jar vigorously until you become tired. Then ask someone else to shake it for a while. After several minutes you will begin to notice that the cream is becoming foamy. Keep shaking until you notice several clumps in a thinner liquid. This is the butter in the buttermilk. Drain the buttermilk into another container. Collect all of the pieces of butter and rinse them with cold water. Then press them together or press them in a small mold. You now have fresh butter to enjoy on a piece of bread or a cracker. You can use the buttermilk to make your favorite pancakes or biscuits if you wish.

WHAT DID WE LEARN?

Is milk an element, a compound or a mixture? (Milk is a mixture.)

What is pasteurization and why is it used on milk? (Pasteurization is the process of heating the milk to kill the bacteria in it.)

What is homogenization and why is it done to milk? (Homogenization is the process that breaks the fat molecules into tiny bits so they stay suspended in the milk. This prevents the cream from separating from the milk and floating to the top.)

What is a foam? (It is a liquid that has air molecules suspended in it.)

TAKING IT FURTHER

Why does cream begin to "weep"? (The fat molecules lose their ability to keep the lighter air molecules trapped and the air eventually escapes.)

Why must cream be churned in order to make butter? (To form butter, the fat molecules must be forced together. Churning forces the molecules to clump together.)

FUN FACT

In 1923 the Federal government passed a law requiring that butter must contain at least 80% milk fat.

FUN FACT

Some milk is pasteurized at a high temperature, 280 °F, for two seconds. This kills all bacteria and allows the milk to be stored at room temperature until it is opened. This is called ultra-high temperature sterilization or UHT.

CLASSIFICATION OF MATTER QUIZ

LESSONS 16-20

Match the word below with its definition or description:

A. Element   B. Compound

C. Mixture   D. Homogeneous

E. Heterogeneous   F. Structural Integrity

G. Pasteurization   H. Water

I. Homogenization   J. Foam

1. _____ A combination of two or more pure substances where each keeps its own properties—a new substance is *not* formed.

2. _____ A liquid with air bubbles trapped in it.

3. _____ A substance made when two or more elements combine chemically.

4. _____ The process of heating a mixture to kill the bacteria in it.

5. _____ A substance that cannot be broken down chemically.

6. _____ A mixture where the substances are thoroughly mixed up.

7. _____ A mixture where the substances are not evenly mixed up.

8. _____ A nearly universal solvent.

9. _____ The process of breaking up fat into tiny pieces that can remain suspended.

10. _____ The ability of fat molecules to keep air molecules suspended.

Short answer:

11. Explain why whipped cream eventually melts into a pool of white liquid?

_____

12. Give an example showing that a compound does not act like the elements that it is made

from. _____

13. Explain why water is considered by many to be a nearly universal solvent.

_____

14. What elements are found in the compound CH_4 _____

SOLUTIONS

WILL IT DISSOLVE?

SUPPLY LIST:

Roll of Lifesavers candy
3 cups
1 copy of "Solutions Experiments" for each child (pg. 78)

Rolling pin
Plastic zipper bag

We have seen that all materials in the universe can be classified into three categories: elements, compounds and mixtures. Mixtures can be further classified as solutions or suspensions. You may think that a solution is an answer to a problem, but in chemistry it means a homogeneous mixture where one substance has been dissolved in another substance. Salt water is a common example of a solution.

In a solution, the substance that is dissolved is called the solute and the substance in which it is dissolved is called the solvent. In the example of salt water, the salt is the solute and the water is the solvent. In a true solution, the solute stays dissolved in the solvent and does not easily come out. If the solute eventually settles to the bottom of the container it is a suspension instead of a true solution. We will discuss suspensions more in the next lesson.

When a solute is dissolved in a solvent, the solvent works to break apart the molecules. As we discussed earlier, water molecules are shaped so that they easily break apart other molecules. A salt crystal is easily broken apart by the movement of the water molecules around it. The tiny salt molecules are then surrounded by water molecules and held away from each other so they cannot recombine. This is what is happening when something is dissolved—its molecules are broken apart from each other and held apart by the solvent.

Solubility is the measure of how much solute can be dissolved in a given amount of solvent. For example, how much salt can be dissolved in

GOD'S DESIGN FOR CHEMISTRY
PROPERTIES OF MATTER

Introduction to Chemistry

Measurement of Matter

States of Matter

Classifications of Matter

Solutions

Food Chemistry

Unit Activity & Conclusion

a cup of water? You can easily dissolve a teaspoon of salt in a cup of water. But if you keep adding salt, eventually there are no longer enough water molecules to surround the salt molecules and some of the salt will not dissolve, but will instead settle on the bottom of the cup. The water is then said to be saturated because it can no longer dissolve any more salt. This does not mean it is no longer a solution; it is just a saturated solution.

The solubility of a solution is affected by temperature. The warmer the liquid the faster the molecules are moving and the more solute it can keep in the solution. You can think of the water as being like a juggler. A juggler can easily keep two or three balls moving through the air. But as more balls are added the juggler must exert more energy to keep them all up. Similarly, in a salt water solution, the water can keep more salt dissolved if it is warmer and has more energy.

How quickly a substance dissolves is also affected by the temperature of the solvent. A warmer liquid will move across the solute more quickly and will thus break the molecules apart more quickly. Warm water molecules move faster than cold water molecules, so warm water will dissolve sugar more quickly than cold water. Also, the amount of surface area exposed to the solvent will affect how quickly the substance dissolves. A sugar cube will dissolve more slowly in a glass of water than a teaspoon of granulated sugar will and powdered sugar will dissolve even faster because more of the sugar molecules are exposed to the water at one time. .

UNDERSTANDING SOLUTIONS:

To help understand how solvents and solutes work together to make a solution, we will dissolve some Lifesaver candies in water. Using a copy of the "Solutions Experiments" worksheet, follow the instructions.

WHAT DID WE LEARN?

What is a solution? (A mixture in which one substance is dissolved in another.)

Is a solution a homogeneous or heterogeneous mixture? (A solution is homogeneous.)

In a solution, what is the name for the substance being dissolved? (The solute)

In a solution, what is the substance called in which the solute is dissolved? (The solvent)

What is solubility? (The amount of a substance that can be dissolved in a given amount of solvent.)

TAKING IT FURTHER

Why can more salt be dissolved in hot water than in cold water? (The warmer molecules are moving faster and can hold more salt molecules away from each other so they can dissolve more salt than the slower, colder water molecules.)

If you want sweet iced tea, would it be better to add the sugar before or after you cool the tea? (If you add the sugar while the tea is hot you will be able to dissolve more sugar and thus the tea will be sweeter. Whether this is better depends on how sweet you like your tea.)

Introduction
to Chemistry

Measurement
of Matter

States of Matter

Classifications
of Matter

Solutions

Food Chemistry

Unit Activity
& Conclusion

Solutions Experiments

Temperature Experiment

Place one Lifesaver candy in each of three cups. Add one cup of cold water to the first cup, one cup of room temperature water to the second cup and one cup of hot tap water to the third cup. Do not stir. Time how long it takes for the Lifesaver to completely dissolve in each cup. Record the times below.

Based on what you learned in the lesson, in which cup do you expect the lifesaver to dissolve most quickly? _____

Temperature of the Water	Time to Dissolve
Cold Water	
Room Temperature Water	
Hot Tap Water	

Was your hypothesis correct? _____

Surface Area Experiment

Place one Lifesaver in a plastic bag and crush it with a rolling pin. Pour all of the pieces of the crushed candy into one cup. Place a whole Lifesaver into a second cup. Pour one cup of hot tap water into each cup. Time how long it takes for the candy to completely dissolve in each cup. Record the times below.

Based on what you learned in the lesson, which Lifesaver do you predict will dissolve most quickly? _____

Surface Area of the Candy	Time to Dissolve
Whole Candy	
Crushed Candy	

Was your hypothesis correct? _____

Tongue Experiment

Will a Lifesaver dissolve on your tongue faster if you move your tongue around or if you keep it still? _____ Try it and see if you are right. Why do you suppose the candy dissolved faster when you moved your tongue? (Because moving your tongue brings more saliva molecules in contact with the candy so they have more opportunity to dissolve it.)

Introduction to Chemistry

Measurement of Matter

States of Matter

Classifications of Matter

Solutions

Food Chemistry

Unit Activity & Conclusion

LESSON 22

SUPENSIONS

AND WE DON'T MEAN GETTING KICKED OUT OF SCHOOL.

SUPPLY LIST:

1 egg
Salt
Dry mustard
Paprika

Vinegar
Vegetable oil
Lemon juice

Have you ever heard the expression, "Oil and water don't mix."? This usually means that two very different people may not get along or two very different ideas may not work well together. This saying comes from the fact that even though many different substances dissolve in water, oil does not dissolve in water. Oil molecules are not easily broken apart by water, so even if you stir the oil and water together they quickly separate. Liquids that do not mix, such as oil and water, are said to be immiscible.

When a mixture is made of one substance that does not dissolve in the other that mixture is called a suspension instead of a solution. The orange juice mixture you tested was a suspension. In a suspension, the molecules of one substance are held apart for a while, but eventually they come back together and settle out. The molecules cannot be broken down small enough for them to stay dissolved. If you leave a container of orange juice alone for a while, much of the pulp will settle to the bottom. That is why most juice bottles say to shake before opening. In the case of oil and water, the oil is lighter than the water so it floats to the top. Either way, the water is not able to keep the molecules in suspension indefinitely.

Even though some substances are immiscible, it is often desirable to have the particles stay in suspension. This can sometimes be accomplished by adding an emulsifier—another substance that helps to keep the suspended particles from coming back together. When baking bread it is

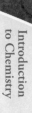

GOD'S DESIGN FOR CHEMISTRY
PROPERTIES OF MATTER

Introduction to Chemistry

Measurement of Matter

States of Matter

Classifications of Matter

Solutions

Food Chemistry

Unit Activity & Conclusion

desirable that the oil be evenly distributed throughout the dough, so an emulsifier is often added to help break up the oil and hold it in suspension in the water. Lecithin, derived from soybeans or other plants, is a common emulsifier added to bread dough. Lecithin can also be derived from egg yolks, and egg yolks are often used as emulsifiers as well. A suspension with very tiny particles throughout the liquid is called a colloid.

A common suspension found in most homes is milk. Milk is mostly water with fat and protein molecules suspended in it. Have you ever seen spoiled milk? As it ages the milk is no longer able to hold the particles in suspension and the solids separate from the liquid. You can separate the milk into its parts by adding 2 tablespoons of vinegar to a cup of milk. This will cause the solids, called curds, to come out of suspension, leaving a watery substance called whey. Do you think Miss Muffet enjoyed her breakfast of curds and whey?

MAKING YOUR OWN SUSPENSION:

Another common suspension is mayonnaise. The main ingredients in mayonnaise are vegetable oil, vinegar and lemon juice. However, if you just mixed those ingredients together you would not get the creamy white spread that so many people love on their sandwiches. In order to make the creamy texture, the oil molecules must be broken into tiny particles and held in suspension in the vinegar and lemon juice. And to keep the molecules from separating back out, an emulsifier must be used. In this case that emulsifier is egg yolk.

Follow the recipe below to make your own homemade mayonnaise:

In a small mixing bowl combine ¼ teaspoon dry mustard, 1/8 teaspoon paprika and ½ teaspoon salt. Add 1 egg yolk and 1 tablespoon vinegar. Beat the mixture at medium speed with an electric mixer until blended. Begin adding 1 cup of vegetable oil by adding it 1 teaspoon at a time, beating constantly. Continue adding oil 1 teaspoon at a time until ¼ cup oil has been added. While continuing to beat, add the remaining ¾ cup of oil in a thin, steady stream, alternating the oil with 1 tablespoon of lemon juice.

Now you can eat this tasty suspension on your lunch. The rest should be refrigerated for up to 4 weeks.

WHAT DID WE LEARN?

What is a suspension? (A suspension is a mixture of substances that don't dissolve. It has particles of one substance that can stay suspended in the other for a short period of time, but not indefinitely.)

What does immiscible mean? (Two liquids that do not mix are immiscible.)

What is an emulsifier? (A substance that allows immiscible liquids to become suspended)

What is a colloid? (A liquid with very tiny particles suspended in it)

TAKING IT FURTHER

What would happen to the mayonnaise if the egg yolk was left out of the recipe? (The oil would separate out and it would lose its creamy texture.)

How is a suspension different from a true solution? (The molecules that are dissolved in a solution will stay dissolved indefinitely, whereas the particles that are suspended will eventually settle out of a suspension if an emulsifier is not added.)

FUN FACT

Many products with oil in them list partially-hydrogenated vegetable oil as an ingredient. Hydrogenation is a process where hydrogen is added to the oil to change the molecular structure of the oil to make it a solid or semi-solid fat. This is a different way to keep oil from separating out of many products.

FUN FACT

Emulsifiers are often used in ice cream to give them a more creamy texture.

Introduction to Chemistry

Measurement of Matter

States of Matter

Classifications of Matter

Solutions

Food Chemistry

Unit Activity & Conclusion

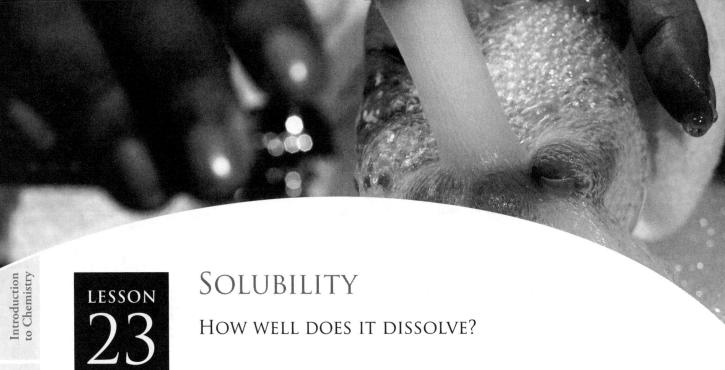

Introduction to Chemistry

Measurement of Matter

States of Matter

Classifications of Matter

Solutions

Food Chemistry

Unit Activity & Conclusion

LESSON 23

SOLUBILITY

HOW WELL DOES IT DISSOLVE?

SUPPLY LIST:

2 cans of soda pop (1 at room temperature and 1 chilled)
2 clear cups

Solubility is the a measure of how well one substance dissolves in another. We generally think of a solid dissolving in a liquid, such as sugar dissolving in water to make sugar water. However, liquids and gases can also be dissolved in liquids. A solution can also be a solid solution if a gas, liquid or other solid is dissolved into a solid, although these are much less common than liquid solutions.

The ability of one substance to dissolve another depends greatly on the design of the molecules of each substance. It is said that, "like dissolves like." What this means is that molecules with similar shapes and structures can dissolve each other better than those with different structures. For example, water does not easily get rid of grease on dirty dishes because the water and oil molecules are very different. However, soap molecules are shaped on one end like a fat or oil molecule and thus are able to break apart the grease molecules on the dishes, while the other end of the soap molecule is similar in shape to a water molecule and can thus be rinsed away.

As you learned in lesson 21, when a liquid or a solid is dissolved in a liquid, the solvent works to keep the molecules of the solute apart from each other and up off the bottom of the container. Because of this, the solubility of the liquid is affected by temperature and pressure. As the temperature rises more solute can be dissolved. Also, as the pressure rises less solute can be dissolved because the pressure forces the molecules to be closer together.

Temperature and pressure have opposite effects on a solution when a gas is dissolved in a liquid. When a gas is dissolved in a liquid, the mol-

GOD'S DESIGN FOR CHEMISTRY

PROPERTIES OF MATTER

Introduction to Chemistry

Measurement of Matter

States of Matter

Classifications of Matter

Solutions

Food Chemistry

Unit Activity & Conclusion

ecules of the solvent are not trying to keep the solute off of the bottom and apart from each other, but they are trying to keep the gas molecules from escaping into the air because the gas molecules are lighter than the liquid molecules. So when the temperature of the solution rises, the molecules speed up and become further apart and allow more of the gas to escape. Thus the solubility of the solution becomes lower as the temperature rises when a gas is dissolved in a liquid. Also, if the pressure increases on the liquid it pushes the molecules closer together so the gas cannot escape as easily and the solubility rises. The idea that solubility of a gas in a liquid increases with pressure is known as Henry's Law and was discovered by William Henry in 1801.

The main factors affecting solubility are the types of molecules involved, the temperature and the pressure of the solution. When a solvent can no longer dissolve any more solute it is said to be saturated. If more solute is added it will settle on the bottom, or if it is a gas, it will escape into the air. Also, if the temperature or pressure change and the solvent can no longer hold all of the solute that was dissolved, some of the solute will come out of the solution. This is called precipitation, and the material that comes out of the solution is called a precipitate. You may have heard the term precipitation referring to rain or snow. This is the same idea. When the clouds can no longer hold all of the water that is in them, some of the water leaves the atmosphere as rain or snow and is called precipitation. When the solution can no longer hold all of its solvent, some of it leaves the solution and is also called precipitation.

WARM OR COLD SOLUTIONS:

Open two cans of soda pop: one that contains cold soda and the other that contains room temperature soda. Pour some soda from each can into a clear cup. (Do not tell your child which cup contains which temperature of soda.) Observe the cups without touching them. Ask the following questions.

1. What solution are you observing? (Carbon dioxide gas dissolved in water. The solution also contains sugar, but we are interested in observing the gas.)

2. Which cup appears to be more bubbly?

3. Does gas escape more easily from a warm solution or a cold solution? (Warm)

4. Which cup contains the colder liquid? (The one with fewer escaping bubbles.)

GOD'S DESIGN FOR CHEMISTRY
PROPERTIES OF MATTER

Introduction to Chemistry

Measurement of Matter

States of Matter

Classifications of Matter

Solutions

Food Chemistry

Unit Activity & Conclusion

Taste the solutions and determine if their hypothesis was correct. The water molecules in the cold soda are moving more slowly than the ones in the warm soda so the cold soda is better able to keep the gas molecules trapped in the pop.

WHAT DID WE LEARN?

What is solubility? (The ability of a solvent to dissolve a solute)

What does "like dissolves like" mean? (Solvents dissolve materials that have similar molecular shapes or structures to them.)

What are the three factors that most affect solubility? (The type of materials being dissolved, temperature and pressure)

What is the name given to particles that come out of a saturated solution? (A precipitate or precipitation)

TAKING IT FURTHER

Why is soda pop canned or bottled at low temperatures and high pressure? (Soda pop is a solution of carbon dioxide dissolved in a liquid. To keep the maximum amount of gas dissolved, the soda is canned or bottled at low temperatures under high pressure.)

Why does a bottle of soda pop eventually go flat once it is opened? (The pressure has been reduced on the solution so the liquid cannot hold as much gas as it once did. The gas escapes into the air and the pop tastes flat.)

If no additional sugar has been added to a saturated solution of sugar water, what can you conclude about the temperature and/or pressure if you notice sugar beginning to settle on the bottom of the cup? (You can conclude that either the temperature of the solution has dropped or the pressure has increased and the water is no longer able to hold all of the sugar in solution.)

Introduction to Chemistry

Measurement of Matter

States of Matter

Classifications of Matter

Solutions

Food Chemistry

Unit Activity & Conclusion

SODA POP

AMERICA'S (SECOND) FAVORITE DRINK

LESSON 24

SUPPLY LIST:

Club soda
Sugar or corn syrup
Vanilla extract
Lemon juice
Food coloring (yellow, red, blue)

Orange juice
Nutmeg
Cinnamon
Baking soda

Americans love soda pop. In fact, after water, it is the most popular drink in the world. People drink 1 billion 8-ounce glasses of soda every day. That is equal to 790 gallons per second! What is it about soda pop that makes it so popular? Not only is it sweet and flavorful, but it has a tangy bubbly taste that results from the carbon dioxide gas that is dissolved in the liquid.

Let's take a look at the process that creates America's favorite soft drink. Soda pop is 90% water. So the process starts with purifying the water that is used to make the pop. Even though the water coming into the manufacturing plant is clean, chemicals are added to the water to remove any flavor from chlorine or other minerals that may be in the water. This is necessary to ensure that the soda made at one plant will taste exactly like the soda made at another plant. The water is tested carefully to make sure it is pure, and then it is passed through a microscopic filter to get rid of any remaining impurities.

The second step in the process is to add a sweetener to the water. 70% of all soda pop is sweetened with corn syrup. The other 30%, diet soda, is sweetened with aspartame or other artificial sweetener. Corn syrup is the cheapest sweetener, so it is the most popular. Corn syrup is produced through an interesting chemical process. Dried corn is soaked in water and sulfuric acid. Then the softened corn is crushed and the endosperm (the

GOD'S DESIGN FOR CHEMISTRY
PROPERTIES OF MATTER

Introduction to Chemistry

Measurement of Matter

States of Matter

Classifications of Matter

Solutions

Food Chemistry

Unit Activity & Conclusion

nutritive tissue within a seed), which contains the starch, is separated from the rest of the corn. An enzyme, a special chemical, is added to liquefy the cornstarch. A second enzyme is added to the liquid to turn it into a sugar called dextrose. But this is not sweet enough for soda pop, so a third enzyme is added to turn the dextrose into a sweeter sugar called fructose. The fructose is boiled to remove the water and the result is a very sweet liquid called high fructose corn syrup. This is the sweetener used in many foods including soda pop.

Diet sodas are sweetened with artificial sweeteners that have significantly fewer calories than corn syrup. The most commonly used artificial sweetener is a chemical called aspartame. Aspartame is a combination of two amino acids and is 200 times sweeter than sugar.

After the water is sweetened, the third step in the soda pop making process is to add flavor and coloring to the liquid. Every brand and flavor of pop has a secret recipe that is carefully guarded by each company. Each flavor is a special blend of herbs, spices, oils, extracts and acids. Cola products are flavored with an extract from the kola nut and are the most popular flavor of soda pop. In fact 70% of all sodas sold are colas. Lemon-lime soda is the second most popular flavor, followed by pepper, root beer and orange soda. All other flavors account for only 2-3% of all soda sales.

In addition to flavorings, color is also added to the liquid. Color is an important step in the process because color affects how we think about the soda. We expect orange flavored soda to have an orange color. We expect cola flavored soda to be brown. So coloring is added to enhance the perceived taste of the product. Once the flavor and color have been added, the liquid is now a finished syrup.

The fourth step in the process is to add the carbonation. The finished syrup is cooled and then sprayed into a pressurized cooler of carbon dioxide. The water in the syrup dissolves the carbon dioxide gas. The carbonated liquid is then put into bottles or cans. The containers are x-rayed for fullness. Then they are warmed up and dried before being packaged in cartons or boxes.

The next time you drink your favorite soda pop, think about the process that is required to produce it.

MAKING YOUR OWN SODA POP:

Although you will not be able to recreate your favorite soda at home, you can make some very tasty soft drinks of your own. Following are two recipes for homemade soda pop.

GOD'S DESIGN FOR CHEMISTRY
PROPERTIES OF MATTER

Introduction to Chemistry

Measurement of Matter

States of Matter

Classifications of Matter

Solutions

Food Chemistry

Unit Activity & Conclusion

Cola

In a large glass, combine the following ingredients:
8 ounces club soda
8 teaspoons sugar or corn syrup
1 teaspoon vanilla extract
1 teaspoon lemon juice
¼ teaspoon orange juice
dash nutmeg
dash cinnamon
4 drops yellow food color
2 drops red food color
2 drops blue food color

Orange (has a somewhat salty taste but can be good)

In a large glass, combine the following ingredients:
6 ounces orange juice
2 ounces water
3 teaspoons sugar or corn syrup
1 teaspoon baking soda (to produce carbon dioxide bubbles)

WHAT DID WE LEARN?

What are the main ingredients of soda pop? (Water, sweetener, flavoring, color, and carbon dioxide)

What is the most popular drink in the world? The second most popular? (Water, followed in second place by soda pop)

What are the two most popular sweeteners used in soda pop? (Corn syrup and aspartame)

TAKING IT FURTHER

Why are soda pop cans warmed and dried before they are boxed? (The soda is very cold when it is canned or bottled. As it warms up, water condenses on the outside of the can or bottle. If this occurred after packaging, the water would make the boxes or cartons soggy, so it is done beforehand.)

Why are recipes for soda pop considered top secret? (People buy a particular brand of pop because they like that flavor better than any other. So if someone obtained a secret recipe the original company could lose money.)

Why would the finished syrup be tested before adding the carbonation? (To ensure that it tastes correctly before it completes the process; to make sure that nothing went wrong in the previous steps.)

GOD'S DESIGN FOR CHEMISTRY
PROPERTIES OF MATTER

Introduction to Chemistry

Measurement of Matter

States of Matter

Classifications of Matter

Solutions

Food Chemistry

Unit Activity & Conclusion

FUN FACT

Some firsts for soft drinks:

- The first soft drink was recorded in the 17th century in France. It was made from lemon, honey and water. It was similar to today's lemonade.

- Carbonation was first added to soft drinks in the 18th century when Jacob Schweppe added carbonation to water in 1794.

- John Pemberton first produced Coca-cola in 1886. Pemberton, a chemist living in Atlanta Georgia, first made Coca-cola as a brain tonic.

FUN FACT

Aspartame was discovered by accident. A scientist had been working with phenylalanine and aspartic acid and some of each ingredient got on his fingers. When he licked his finger to turn the page of a book, he noticed that it tasted sweet and thus aspartame was born.

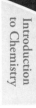

Introduction to Chemistry

Measurement of Matter

States of Matter

Classifications of Matter

Solutions

Food Chemistry

Unit Activity & Conclusion

CONCENTRATION

HOW SALTY IS THE SALT WATER?

SUPPLY LIST:

Milk   Ice
Sugar   Salt
Vanilla extract   Quart-sized plastic zipper bag
Sandwich-sized plastic zipper bag

Have you ever tasted Kool-Aid that was too weak or lemonade that was too strong? Both of these drinks are solutions and as you learned, a solution could have a very small amount of solute dissolved in it or it could have enough solute to saturate the solution. If there is a relatively small amount of solute in the solution it is said to be dilute. This would be the Kool-Aid that tastes watered down. If it has a relatively large amount of solute, the solution is said to be concentrated. This would be the very strong lemonade.

Dilute and concentrated are both qualitative descriptions of the concentration of solute in a solution. As we learned in earlier lessons, qualitative descriptions can be helpful, but quantitative measurements are often more helpful. The quantitative measurement of the concentration of a solution measures the number of grams of solute dissolved in 100 grams of solution. For example, if 5 grams of sugar are dissolved in 95 grams of water the resulting 100 grams of sugar water is said to be a 5% sugar solution. This quantitative measurement is necessary to enable scientists to be able to repeat results of experiments.

Other than getting the right concentration in your soft drink, there are many reasons for changing the concentration of a solution. Increasing the concentration of a liquid solution generally raises its boiling point and lowers its freezing point. The boiling point of the solution is higher than pure water because the dissolved molecules get in the way of the water molecules

GOD'S DESIGN FOR CHEMISTRY
PROPERTIES OF MATTER

Introduction to Chemistry

Measurement of Matter

States of Matter

Classifications of Matter

Solutions

Food Chemistry

Unit Activity & Conclusion

and make it harder for the water molecules to reach the surface and escape into the air. Thus it takes more energy to make the solution boil. This can be very useful in an engine where you want to cool the engine without boiling away the liquid that is absorbing the heat. In order to make the engine in your car work better, antifreeze is added to the water in the radiator. This allows the solution of water and antifreeze to absorb heat from the engine and not boil over.

Similarly, antifreeze keeps the water in your radiator from freezing, even when the temperature is below 32 °F—the freezing point of water. In order for water to freeze, the molecules must line up and form crystals. In a solution, the solute keeps the water molecules separated and makes it harder for the water to freeze. Therefore, the temperature must get much colder before the solution will freeze. This helps your car engine keep running even in very cold weather. Another important application of solutions is the sprinkling of salt on sidewalks in the snow. The salt molecules become dissolved in the water and this lowers the temperature at which the water freezes so it is less likely that ice will form on the sidewalk.

MAKING ICE CREAM:

One very fun application of a salt water solution is used in the making of ice cream. Salt is added to the ice that surrounds the ice cream container. The salt lowers the freezing point of the water and thus allows it to absorb more heat from the ice cream mixture, causing the cream mixture to freeze more quickly. To observe this first-hand do the following.

In a small sandwich-sized plastic zipper bag combine:

½ cup milk
1 Tablespoon sugar
1/8 teaspoon vanilla extract

Zip the bag shut and make sure it is sealed.

Place the small bag inside a larger zipper bag. Add 2 cups of ice cubes and 2 teaspoons of salt. Zip the larger bag closed. Shake the bags for several minutes until the milk mixture freezes. If it does not seem to be freezing after several minutes, add another teaspoon of salt to the ice mixture.

GOD'S DESIGN FOR CHEMISTRY
PROPERTIES OF MATTER

Introduction to Chemistry

Measurement of Matter

States of Matter

Classifications of Matter

Solutions

Food Chemistry

Unit Activity & Conclusion

When the milk mixture is frozen, remove the small bag. Carefully wipe off the salt water from the outside of the bag, and then open it and enjoy your sweet dessert!

WHAT DID WE LEARN?

What is a dilute solution? (One in which there are relatively few solute molecules in the solution.)

What is a concentrated solution? (One in which there are a relatively large number of solute molecules in the solution.)

How does the concentration of a solution affect its boiling point? (In general, the more concentrated it is, the higher the boiling point will be.)

How does the concentration of a solution affect its freezing point? (In general, the more concentrated it is, the lower the freezing point will be.)

TAKING IT FURTHER

Why is a quantitative measurement for solubility usually more useful than a qualitative measurement? (Qualitative measurements are based on people's perceptions and not easily repeated. One person may think that the lemonade is too strong while another thinks it is too weak. But quantitative measurements are not a matter of opinion and can be repeated.)

If a little antifreeze helps an engine run better, would it be better to add straight antifreeze to the radiator? (Not necessarily. The combination of different molecules raises the boiling point and lowers the freezing point of both substances in the solution, but straight antifreeze would not necessarily have the same effect.)

Introduction to Chemistry

Measurement of Matter

States of Matter

Classifications of Matter

Solutions

Food Chemistry

Unit Activity & Conclusion

LESSON 26

SEAWATER

THE WORLD'S MOST COMMON SOLUTION

SUPPLY LIST:

Water
Salt

Soda Straw
Egg

As we have already learned, a solution is formed when one substance is dissolved in another substance. We have also learned that water is one of the best solvents around. Because of this, when rain falls and water flows over the surface of the earth, the water dissolves many minerals that are found on the ground. These minerals are carried into streams and rivers and eventually end up in the oceans. Therefore, seawater, which covers about 71% of the surface of the earth, is the largest and most common solution in the world.

The most common mineral dissolved in seawater is salt. But many other minerals are found there as well. Magnesium and bromide, along with sodium chloride (table salt) are available in high enough concentrations in seawater to be removed and sold commercially. All together, there are 55 different elements that have been identified in seawater. In 1000 grams of water there are about 35 grams of minerals. Of the minerals in the seawater, about 75% is salt, although the salt concentration varies from place to place. This gives seawater a salt concentration of about 3%; 3 grams of salt in 100 grams of seawater.

In addition to minerals, gases such as oxygen, nitrogen and carbon dioxide are also dissolved in the water. The concentration of oxygen is highest near the surface of the ocean. Some oxygen dissolves from the air into the water, but most of it is produced by plants, primarily algae, that grow near the surface of the water.

The ocean is a wonderful solution of water, minerals and gases that God has provided to support life on earth.

MAKING SEAWATER:

You can make your own seawater solution. Start with one cup of water. Add 1¼ teaspoons of salt. Stir until the salt is dissolved. This makes a solution that is about 3% salt water. Next, dissolve gases in the water by gently blowing air bubbles through a straw into the water for about 15 seconds. The air coming out of your lungs contains oxygen, nitrogen and carbon dioxide—the three most common gases that are found in seawater. You now have a solution that is very close to the composition of seawater. Actual seawater has other minerals in it, but they are usually found in very small quantities, so your solution is very close to actual seawater.

Seawater is more dense than freshwater so you will be more buoyant in the ocean than in a swimming pool. In fact, many people like to swim in the Great Salt Lake in Utah because it is even saltier than the ocean, thus making it easy to float in. To demonstrate this, carefully place an egg in a cup of fresh water. What happens? (It sinks to the bottom.) Now place the egg in your seawater. Does it float above the bottom of the cup? The egg should float. If it does not, remove the egg and add an additional teaspoon of salt, then try it again.

WHAT DID WE LEARN?

What is the most common solution on earth? (Seawater)

What are the main elements found in the ocean besides water? (Sodium chloride—salt, magnesium and bromine.)

How does salt get into the ocean? (Water flowing over land dissolves salt and other minerals and carries them to the ocean. The minerals stay behind when the water evaporates.)

Name one gas that is dissolved in the ocean water? (Oxygen is the main gas. Nitrogen, carbon dioxide and other gases are present as well.)

TAKING IT FURTHER

Why is seawater saltier than water in the rivers and lakes? (Fresh water is continually entering and exiting the rivers and lakes. So the amount of salt remains low. However, in the ocean, the only way that water leaves is through evaporation, which removes the water but leaves the minerals. After thousands of years, the salt has built up in the oceans.)

Why is there more oxygen near the surface of the ocean than in deeper parts? (Algae and other plants grow near the surface and produce oxygen that dissolves in the water.)

Introduction to Chemistry

Measurement of Matter

States of Matter

Classifications of Matter

Solutions

Food Chemistry

Unit Activity & Conclusion

DESALINATION OF WATER

Desalination is the process of removing salt from ocean water to produce fresh water. Many places in the world do not have enough fresh water for drinking, irrigating and manufacturing. While other areas have more than enough water, the cost of transporting it is too great. Therefore, many people are trying to find ways to take salt water from the ocean and turn it in to fresh water.

One way that this is done is through distillation. Distillation is a process in which water is heated until it evaporates, leaving the salt and other minerals behind. The steam is then allowed to condense in another container to form fresh water. One of the earliest recorded uses of distillation occurred around 50 B.C. when the armies of Julius Caesar made distillation devices using the sun's heat to evaporate water from the Mediterranean Sea. These units were small and therefore could only make small amounts of fresh water. In addition to distillation, man is exploring reverse osmosis, electrodialysis and vacuum freezing as other desalination processes. Reverse osmosis is the most common of these. Reverse osmosis forces water through a membrane that only allows water molecules to pass and blocks all the larger molecules. One osmosis process uses hollow membrane spheres that are pulled under the surface of the ocean. The water pressure of the ocean forces water into the sphere, while the membrane blocks the salt and other minerals, leaving them outside the sphere.

One group of people that has always been interested in desalination is sailors. To combat the fear of dying at sea for lack of fresh water, many different ideas were developed to turn salt water into fresh water. In 1791, Thomas Jefferson, then Secretary of State, had a technical report printed on the back of all papers on board the ships describing how to use distillation as a source of fresh water, in case of an emergency. Later, steam ships used distillation units to make the fresh water for their boilers from seawater. This reduced the cost of running steam ships by allowing the cargo bays to carry cargo instead of fresh water. By the time of World War II, mobile desalination units were in wide use. Because of many fresh water shortages after World War II, governments and private parties around the world began working to find ways to reduce the costs of desalination, while increasing production.

Today, there are more then 7,500 desalination plants in use around the world. 60% of these plants are located in the Middle East. One of the largest plants in use today is in Saudi Arabia, which produces around 128,000,000 gallons of fresh water each day. About 12% of the desalination plants are in the Americas, mostly in Florida and the Caribbean.

Introduction to Chemistry

Measurement of Matter

States of Matter

Classifications of Matter

Solutions

Food Chemistry

Unit Activity & Conclusion

WATER TREATMENT

MAKING IT CLEAN

SUPPLY LIST:

Empty 2-liter soda bottle
Sand
Charcoal briquettes
Cotton balls
Dish or tray
Alum

Dirt
Gravel or small pebbles
Plastic zipper bag
Hammer
Goggles

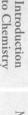

Because water is a nearly universal solvent, many substances become dissolved in it. This can be very useful if you are trying to wash away dirt or other substances. However, this can be very bad if you are trying to obtain good drinking water. Most water we use today comes from rivers, lakes and streams. This water is not clean enough to be safe to drink because of the substances dissolved in it as well as the particles suspended in it. Therefore, most towns and cities have freshwater treatment facilities that clean up the water and remove unwanted and harmful substances before the water gets to your house.

The first stage in water treatment is called sedimentation. The water is placed in a large holding tank and large particles are allowed to settle to the bottom. These particles are not actually dissolved in the water but are suspended by the movement of the water. When the water sits still for a length of time, these particles fall to the bottom of the tank and are removed.

The water is then sent through a filter that removes most smaller particles that are still suspended in the water. The water then goes to a mixing basin where chemicals are added to the water. Chlorine is added to kill bacteria and to eliminate odors in the water. Fluoride is added to the water in many cities to help strengthen teeth. And alum is added because it causes any remaining particles to clump together. This water is sent to another

95

GOD'S DESIGN FOR CHEMISTRY
PROPERTIES OF MATTER

Introduction
to Chemistry

Measurement
of Matter

States of Matter

Classifications
of Matter

Solutions

Food Chemistry

Unit Activity
& Conclusion

settling basin where the remaining particles precipitate out and fall to the bottom of the tank and are scraped away.

Finally, the water is sent through a filter to eliminate any remaining unwanted particles. The filter usually consists of a layer of gravel, then a layer of charcoal, then a layer of sand. In some treatment facilities a final amount of chlorine is added to the water and then it is released into the main water pipes where it flows to homes and other buildings for people to use.

After the water is used in homes and offices, the water in most areas goes into the sewage system where it flows to the wastewater treatment facility. Because used water often has bacteria and other harmful substances in it, it needs to be cleaned up before it is returned to the streams and rivers.

At a wastewater treatment facility the water first flows through a series of bars that trap large objects and remove them from the water. Next, the water is placed in a holding tank where smaller particles settle to the bottom. The water is then drained away leaving behind a slimy layer on the bottom of the tank called sludge. The sludge is treated with a helpful type of bacteria that kills the harmful bacteria and is then spread on fields and used as fertilizer. The water is also treated with a type of bacteria that eats harmful bacteria and dirt. The water is then sent to another holding tank and then released into a river or stream.

This cleaned water is then safe for wildlife, although it may not be safe for human consumption. It is important that we keep our water clean so that we do not harm wildlife or people. Water can become polluted when people dump harmful chemicals, oil or other dangerous substances in the water. These items need to be disposed of in a responsible matter so that we are good stewards of the world God has given us.

CLEANING OUR WATER:

You can make your own mini-water treatment plant. First you need to make a filter. Have an adult cut off the bottom of a 2-liter soda bottle. Next, tightly stuff the top or mouth of the bottle with cotton balls. Turn the bottle upside down and add ½ cup of sand to the bottle.

Place 3 charcoal briquettes in a plastic zipper bag. While wearing goggles or other eye protection, use a hammer to break the charcoal into small pieces. Place these pieces in the bottle on top of the sand. Next, add a layer two inches thick of small gravel or pebbles.

Now you need to make some dirty water. Add a small amount of dirt to a cup of water and stir thoroughly. Pour ¼ of the water into another

GOD'S DESIGN FOR CHEMISTRY
PROPERTIES OF MATTER

Introduction to Chemistry

Measurement of Matter

States of Matter

Classifications of Matter

Solutions

Food Chemistry

Unit Activity & Conclusion

container for later comparison. Allow the rest of the water to settle for 5 minutes and notice that much of the dirt settles to the bottom. Pour this water into another cup; be sure not to pour the sediment into the cup. Next, add 1 teaspoon of alum to the water. Stir for thirty seconds and again allow the water to settle for 5 minutes. Notice that more of the particles have clumped together and settled to the bottom. Now, have someone hold your bottle filter over a dish or cup and carefully pour most of the water into the bottle. Be sure not to pour any of the particles from the bottom of the container into the filter. Allow the water to drip through the filter. Compare the water that comes out of the filter with the original water you saved. The filtered water should be much cleaner. Even though this water looks clean, do **not** drink it. It still may contain harmful bacteria.

WHAT DID WE LEARN?

Why do we need water treatment plants? (Water from rivers and lakes contains dirt, harmful bacteria and other substances that are not healthy for people to drink.)

What are the three main things that are done to water to make it clean enough for human consumption? (Particles are allowed to settle out, chemicals are added to kill bacteria and the water is filtered.)

Why is it important not to dump harmful chemicals into rivers and lakes? (The chemicals will dissolve in the water and harm the plants and animals living there.)

TAKING IT FURTHER

How is the filter you built similar to God's design for cleaning the water? (Much of the water that falls on the earth sinks into the ground where it flows through sand and gravel and becomes more pure before reaching rivers and underground water tables.)

FUN FACT

Some homes are not connected to a sewer system. Instead, they have septic systems that filter out large particles and then allow the wastewater from the homes to flow into the ground where the natural filter of the soil, sand and rocks purifies the water before it enters the water table.

FUN FACT

The first recorded case of man trying to improve his water supply is in Exodus, when the Israelites are at Marah. God had Moses throw a tree branch into the water to make the bitter water sweet. Other examples include drawings dating back to around 1400 B.C. showing Egyptians using sedimentation methods to improve their drinking water. And around 500 B.C. Hippocrates invented a special cloth called the "Hippocrates Sleeve" to strain rainwater.

SOLUTIONS QUIZ

LESSONS 21-27

Answer True or False for each statement below.

1. _____ All solutions are mixtures.

2. _____ All mixtures are solutions.

3. _____ A saturated solution can dissolve more solute.

4. _____ True solutions do not settle out.

5. _____ Milk is a true solution.

6. _____ Temperature affects how fast substances dissolve.

7. _____ Surface area affects how fast substances dissolve.

8. _____ A dilute solution has a high amount of solute.

9. _____ The boiling point of a solution is affected by concentration.

10. _____ Cold liquids can suspend more gas than warmer liquids.

Short answer.

11. Describe why increased pressure decreases the solubility of a solid in a liquid.

    _____

12. Describe why increased pressure increases the solubility of a gas in a liquid.

    _____

13. What is a precipitate? _____

14. Why is salt added to ice when freezing ice cream? _____

15. What is likely to happen to a car without antifreeze in the radiator? _____

    _____

Introduction to Chemistry

Measurement of Matter

States of Matter

Classifications of Matter

Solutions

Food Chemistry

Unit Activity & Conclusion

FOOD CHEMISTRY

YOU ARE WHAT YOU EAT

SUPPLY LIST:

Ingredients to make your favorite cookies

One of the most interesting places to learn about chemistry is in the kitchen. Our bodies are made up of a very complex collection of chemicals, and the food we eat is a collection of chemicals. So there are a lot of chemicals to be found in the kitchen. The first place to begin looking for chemicals is on food labels. Foods consist of three major types of chemicals: carbohydrates, proteins and fats. So these three items will be listed on most food labels.

Carbohydrates are molecules made from carbon, oxygen and hydrogen. There are two types of carbohydrates: sugars and starches. Sugars naturally occur in many fruits and vegetables. Starches are found in wheat, rice, oats, other grains and potatoes. Good places to find foods with carbohydrates are in a loaf of bread and a box of cereal. Natural sugar is found in many foods containing fruits and vegetables, but sugar is also added to many other foods as well, including many breakfast cereals. When you look at the list of ingredients don't be fooled. Sugars are called by many names, so even if the list does not include the word "sugar" the food may still have carbohydrates from sugar. You can look for words like sucrose, fructose or high fructose corn syrup. These are different types of sugar.

To find proteins you can look for foods that contain meat, nuts and many types of beans such as navy, pinto or black beans. Proteins are also found in many dairy products such as milk, cheese and ice cream. Proteins are made from molecules called amino acids that consist of carbon, hydrogen, oxygen and nitrogen atoms.

Fats are very long molecules that are found in many foods. Fats are found in nuts, meats and many dairy products. Fats can also be found in

GOD'S DESIGN FOR CHEMISTRY
PROPERTIES OF MATTER

Introduction to Chemistry

Measurement of Matter

States of Matter

Classifications of Matter

Solutions

Food Chemistry

Unit Activity & Conclusion

many vegetables. Fats are also found in many snack foods and anything made with oil, margarine or butter.

Food chemistry does not end with the carbohydrates, proteins and fats. There are many other chemicals in our food. First, foods also contain vitamins and minerals, which are all chemical compounds. Second, many foods have chemicals added to them such as preservatives, flavor enhancers and color enhancers. Finally, some chemicals are added to foods to change their texture. For example, baking soda and baking powder are added to cakes, cookies and other baked items to make them lighter and fluffier.

So look around your kitchen and you will find a whole chemistry lab just waiting to be explored.

BAKING SODA – A VITAL CHEMICAL:

To demonstrate the importance of chemical reactions in our foods you can make two sets of cookies; one with baking soda and one without. Baking soda is a chemical called sodium bicarbonate. Baking soda is a base and it reacts with an acid. This chemical reaction releases gas bubbles.

First, make your favorite cookie dough following the recipe, except leave out the baking soda. Place three cookies on the baking pan. Now add the baking soda to the remaining cookie dough and mix thoroughly. Bake all of the cookies according to the recipe. Be sure to keep track of which cookies have baking soda and which do not.

After baking the cookies, first observe the cookies. How do the cookies with baking soda look compared to the cookies without baking soda? Are there differences in color, shape or texture? Next, taste one cookie from each batch of dough. What differences do you notice? Which cookies taste better?

WHAT DID WE LEARN?

What are the three main types of chemicals that naturally occur in food? (Carbohydrates, proteins and fats)

What kinds of chemicals are often added to foods? (Preservatives, flavor enhancers and color enhancers.)

Why is the kitchen a great place to look for chemicals? (All of our foods are made of chemicals and many chemical reactions occur as we are cooking.)

TAKING IT FURTHER

If you eat a peanut butter and jelly sandwich which part of the sandwich will be providing the most carbohydrates? The most fat? The most protein? (The bread will provide the most carbohydrates, although it depends on how much jelly you put on. Jelly is mostly sugar, which is also a carbohydrate. The peanut butter will provide nearly all of the fat and most of the protein.)

GOD'S DESIGN FOR CHEMISTRY
PROPERTIES OF MATTER

Introduction to Chemistry

Measurement of Matter

States of Matter

Classifications of Matter

Solutions

Food Chemistry

Unit Activity & Conclusion

FUN FACT

The food pyramid shows recommended daily servings of each food group. The foods are grouped according to the major chemicals or nutrients they contain.

MyPyramid
STEPS TO A HEALTHIER YOU
MyPyramid.gov

GRAINS	VEGETABLES	FRUITS	MILK	MEAT & BEANS

GRAINS Make half your grains whole	VEGETABLES Vary your veggies	FRUITS Focus on fruits	MILK Get your calcium-rich foods	MEAT & BEANS Go lean with protein
Eat at least 3 oz. of whole-grain cereals, breads, crackers, rice, or pasta every day 1 oz. is about 1 slice of bread, about 1 cup of breakfast cereal, or ½ cup of cooked rice, cereal, or pasta	Eat more dark-green veggies like broccoli, spinach, and other dark leafy greens Eat more orange vegetables like carrots and sweetpotatoes Eat more dry beans and peas like pinto beans, kidney beans, and lentils	Eat a variety of fruit Choose fresh, frozen, canned, or dried fruit Go easy on fruit juices	Go low-fat or fat-free when you choose milk, yogurt, and other milk products If you don't or can't consume milk, choose lactose-free products or other calcium sources such as fortified foods and beverages	Choose low-fat or lean meats and poultry Bake it, broil it, or grill it Vary your protein routine — choose more fish, beans, peas, nuts, and seeds

For a 2,000-calorie diet, you need the amounts below from each food group. To find the amounts that are right for you, go to MyPyramid.gov.

Eat 6 oz. every day	Eat 2½ cups every day	Eat 2 cups every day	Get 3 cups every day; for kids aged 2 to 8, it's 2	Eat 5½ oz. every day

Find your balance between food and physical activity
- Be sure to stay within your daily calorie needs.
- Be physically active for at least 30 minutes most days of the week.
- About 60 minutes a day of physical activity may be needed to prevent weight gain.
- For sustaining weight loss, at least 60 to 90 minutes a day of physical activity may be required.
- Children and teenagers should be physically active for 60 minutes every day, or most days.

Know the limits on fats, sugars, and salt (sodium)
- Make most of your fat sources from fish, nuts, and vegetable oils.
- Limit solid fats like butter, stick margarine, shortening, and lard, as well as foods that contain these.
- Check the Nutrition Facts label to keep saturated fats, trans fats, and sodium low.
- Choose food and beverages low in added sugars. Added sugars contribute calories with few, if any, nutrients.

MyPyramid.gov
STEPS TO A HEALTHIER YOU

U.S. Department of Agriculture
Center for Nutrition Policy and Promotion
April 2005
CNPP-15

Introduction to Chemistry

Measurement of Matter

States of Matter

Classifications of Matter

Solutions

Food Chemistry

Unit Activity & Conclusion

LESSON 29

CHEMICAL ANALYSIS OF FOOD

HOW DO I KNOW WHAT I'M EATING?

SUPPLY LIST:

1 copy of the "Chemical Analysis Worksheet" for each child (pg. 104)
Iodine
Brown paper bag
Bread
Vegetable oil

Potato or tortilla chips
Apple slices
Flour
Peanut butter

The main chemicals that naturally occur in food are carbohydrates, proteins and fats. Foods also contain water, vitamins and minerals. If you look at the labels on most foods, they will tell you how many grams of carbohydrates, protein and fat are in each serving. The label will probably also tell you which vitamins and minerals are present in the food. This information can be very helpful in deciding which foods to eat and which foods to avoid. You may want to limit the amount of salt or fat in your diet and food labels can help you do that. But how did the manufacturer of the food determine the chemical composition of the food?

Scientists have designed many tests that help determine the chemical composition of food. Some of these can be done easily at home. Others require special chemicals and equipment that are not readily available. A simple way to detect the presence of fats, particularly fats that are in the form of oil, is called the brown paper test. If you place a sample of food that contains oil on a piece of brown paper, like a shopping bag or lunch bag, the oil will cause the paper to become translucent; it will allow light to pass through it. If the sample only contains water, the paper will not be translucent, but will only look darker. It's simple to test for the presence of fats.

Testing for carbohydrates and proteins is a little more difficult. There are two kinds of carbohydrates in foods: sugars and starches. The element iodine will chemically combine with starch molecules to form a substance

GOD'S DESIGN FOR CHEMISTRY
PROPERTIES OF MATTER

Introduction to Chemistry

Measurement of Matter

States of Matter

Classifications of Matter

Solutions

Food Chemistry

Unit Activity & Conclusion

that changes from the red/orange of the iodine to a blue color. This is a quick test for starch. A substance that is used to detect the presence of another substance, usually by changing color, is called a reagent. Iodine is a reagent used to test for starch. Other reagents are used to test for other chemicals. Benedict's solution is a reagent used to test for glucose or sugar. Biuret solution is used to test for the presence of protein, and indophenol solution is used to test for vitamin C. You probably don't have most of these reagents in your home, so it is more difficult to test for some of these chemicals. Chemists use many other chemicals to test for various substances by examining the results of various chemical reactions. These tests enable scientists to make food labels that tell us what is in our food so we can make good choices about the foods we eat.

ANALYZING YOUR FOOD:

Complete the "Chemical Analysis Worksheet."
(Foods with oil: vegetable oil, peanut butter, chips. Foods with starch: bread, flour)

WHAT DID WE LEARN?

What are the main chemicals listed on food labels? (Carbohydrates such as sugar and starch, proteins, fats, vitamins and minerals.)

How do food manufacturers know what to put on their labels? (Chemists have tested the foods to see what they are composed of.)

What is one way to test if a food contains oil? (Place a sample on brown paper for a few minutes and see if it makes the paper become translucent.)

What is a reagent? (A substance that is used to detect the presence of a particular chemical.)

TAKING IT FURTHER

How do you suppose reagents work? (Usually the reagent molecules react with the desired chemical to produce a substance that is a different color from the reagent. For example, iodine turns blue in the presence of starch molecules.)

Why is it important to know what chemicals are in our food? (This information allows us to compare different foods and decide which ones are best to eat. Also, some people are allergic to particular foods and food labels help them avoid those foods.)

CHEMICAL ANALYSIS WORKSHEET

TESTING FOR OILS

Step 1: Place a sample of each of the foods listed on the chart below on a piece of brown paper. Write the name of the sample next to it on the paper. Allow to sit for 5 minutes.

Step 2: Wipe off any excess sample that has not dried or evaporated.

Step 3: Hold the paper up to the light and notice which samples caused the paper to become translucent (allow light to pass through). Write your observations below.

Step 4: Check the food label (if available) to see if oil is listed in the ingredients. Write your answers below.

Step 5: Write whether you believe each sample tested has oil in it or not.

Sample type	Translucent?	Oil listed in ingredients?	Oil in this sample?
Water			
Vegetable Oil			
Peanut butter			
Potato or tortilla chips			
Apple slice			

TESTING FOR STARCH

Step 1: Test each of the foods listed on the chart below for the presence of starch by placing a drop of iodine on each sample.

Step 2: Record the color of the iodine after it combines with the food. Blue indicates starch.

Step 3: Check the food label (if available) to see if grains such as wheat, rice or barley are listed in the ingredients. Write your answers below.

Step 4: Write whether you believe each sample tested has starch in it or not.

Sample type	Color of iodine/food combination	Grain listed in the ingredients?	Starch in this sample?
Water			
Bread			
Apple slice			
Flour			

LESSON 30

FLAVORS

CHOCOLATE OR VANILLA?

SUPPLY LIST:

Instant pudding mix (your favorite flavor)
Milk

What is your favorite flavor of ice cream? For most Americans it is chocolate or vanilla. Flavor is a combination of taste and smell. Flavors are chemical compounds that stimulate the taste buds in your mouth and the olfactory (smell) receptors in your nose. When you take a bite of ice cream or a swallow of juice, food molecules touch your taste buds and gas molecules go into your nasal cavity to allow you to fully enjoy the flavor.

God has created a nearly endless variety of flavors. Many are very pleasant and others are very unpleasant. The chemicals that produce the flavors we like may be present in only certain parts of a plant or may only be present when the fruit is ripe. Some plants must be heated to develop the flavor. This process is called fermentation.

Herbs are plant leaves that are used to add flavor to our cooking. Some common herbs you may find in your kitchen are basil, oregano, parsley and sage. Herbs can be used fresh, but often the leave are dried and crushed so they can be stored and used as needed.

Spices are flavors that come from roots, stems and seeds of plants. Some common spices include pepper, cinnamon and nutmeg. In the past, spices and other natural flavors have been very expensive. In fact, finding a new trade route to India and China, where most of the spices were grown, was one reason Columbus sailed west across the Atlantic Ocean. However, most flavors are much more affordable today than in the middle ages. Scientists have learned to isolate the desired chemical compounds and concentrate them. You can buy vanilla or almond extract and have access to these flavors

105

GOD'S DESIGN FOR CHEMISTRY
PROPERTIES OF MATTER

Introduction to Chemistry

Measurement of Matter

States of Matter

Classifications of Matter

Solutions

Food Chemistry

Unit Activity & Conclusion

much more easily today than you could have 200-400 years ago.

In addition to natural flavors, scientists have learned to recreate many

flavors by copying the chemical composition of particular flavors. They have also learned to make new chemical combinations that have flavors without any natural counterpart, including bubble gum, spice and smoke flavors. Artificial flavors are usually less expensive than the natural flavors they are replacing. However, even though the artificial flavor may have the same chemical formula as the natural flavor, the experienced tongue can usually tell the difference.

So the next time you enjoy your favorite ice cream, thank God for the wonderful way He created the flavors as well as the wonderful way He created your body to enjoy the chemicals in your food.

ENJOYING YOUR FAVORITE FLAVOR:

You can enjoy your favorite flavor by mixing your favorite flavor of instant pudding with milk then eating it together.

WHAT DID WE LEARN?

What two parts of your body are needed in order to fully enjoy the flavor of your food? (The taste buds in your mouth and the smell receptors in your nose)

What is the difference between an herb and a spice? (Herbs come from the leaves of a plant; spices come from other parts of the plant.)

What is the difference between a natural flavor and an artificial flavor? (Natural flavors come directly from a plant. Artificial flavors are created by combining chemicals in a lab or factory.)

TAKING IT FURTHER

Why might a cook prefer to use fresh herbs rather than dried herbs? (Fresh herbs usually have a milder flavor than dried herbs.

However, fresh herbs can spoil more quickly than dried herbs.)

Why do you think artificial vanilla tastes different than natural vanilla even though they have the same chemical formula? (Flavor is a complicated thing. Scientists are not quite sure how the flavors are changed, but artificial flavors often produce an unpleasant or bitter aftertaste that natural flavors do not have.)

FUN FACT

There are about 200 natural flavors and 750 artificial flavors used in the food industry today.

Introduction to Chemistry

Measurement of Matter

States of Matter

Classifications of Matter

Solutions

Food Chemistry

Unit Activity & Conclusion

CHOCOLATE AND VANILLA

What do Europeans eat twice as much of as Americans? The answer is chocolate. Americans eat an average of 11 pounds of chocolate per person per year, but Europeans eat more than 22 pounds of chocolate per person per year.

Two of the most popular flavors in the world are chocolate and vanilla. Because cacao trees and vanilla plants only grow in tropical areas, both of these flavors were known to the inhabitants of Mexico and South America long before the Europeans discovered their wonderful properties. But with the Spanish discovery of the New World, these flavors were taken to the Old World where they quickly become extremely popular.

The word vanilla comes from the Spanish word for little pod and was so named by Cortez in 1519. Vanilla flavoring is widely used in sweets, cough syrups, medicines and is almost always found in chocolate flavored items. The Aztecs are credited with being the first to combine the delicious flavors of chocolate and vanilla. And the Spanish took these flavors back to Europe.

In 1602, a doctor named Hugh Morgan, made a medicine for Queen Elizabeth that was flavored with vanilla. This is believed to be the first European use of vanilla by itself, without chocolate, and led to the use of vanilla as a separate flavor in it own right. Queen Elizabeth was so taken with vanilla that it is recorded that later in life she refused to eat foods that were not flavored with vanilla. Today, vanilla can be found in nearly every American and European household. America imports about three million pounds of vanilla every year.

Vanilla flavoring comes from the pods of the vanilla plant. These 5-10 inch long pods are long and slender, and look somewhat like green beans when they are on the plant. The vanilla pods are the fruit of the orchid-like flowers on the plant. On vanilla plantations, the flowers are hand pollinated to ensure the best results.

Once the pods are ready to be picked, the process required to fully develop the desired flavor takes about six months. This process is called fermentation and requires several steps. First, the pods are placed in the sun and heated to start the fermentation process. Next, they

are folded in blankets and allowed to sweat over night. Sometimes this heating and sweating process is repeated. Next, the pods are removed from the blankets and allowed to dry in the sun for several weeks. When completely dry, the pods are placed in boxes and aged for 2-3 months.

Once the pods are aged they are sorted, packaged and shipped to various countries where they are sold to bakeries and food processing plants. Most often the pods are soaked in alcohol to concentrate the flavor into vanilla extract, which is then used in many recipes.

Even more popular than vanilla is chocolate, which comes from the cacao beans that grow on the cacao tree. The name cacao comes from the Aztec word cacahautl, which was a chocolate drink enjoyed by the Aztecs. But unlike the hot cocoa of today, this drink was spiced with vanilla and peppers and did not contain sugar.

Cacao trees grow only in the tropics. They cannot grow at altitudes above 300 feet or in temperatures below 60 °F. The trees also require at least 50 inches of rainfall each year, as well as an atmosphere with high humidity. These conditions only occur in a very limited part of the world so cacao trees are only grown in a few places.

Cacao flowers are pollinated by the midge, a small mosquito-like fly. Once pollinated, the flowers produce football shaped pods that are about 10 inches long and 3-4 inches around. Each pod contains 20-40 seeds. Once the pods are ripe they are picked and then experience a process very much like the fermentation process for the vanilla pods. However, the process of turning cacao beans into cocoa is more complicated.

First, the pods are cut open and the flesh and seeds are scooped into a box that is placed in the sun and allowed to ferment for 5-7 days. The fermentation causes the flavor to begin to develop in the seeds. During this process the pulp turns to a liquid and drains away and the seeds begin to dry.

After curing, the seeds are roasted at a temperature between 225-300 °F for 15-20 minutes. Next, the seeds are cracked open and the seed coats are removed. The seeds are crushed producing a cocoa butter solution. When cooled, this becomes chocolate liquor, which is baking chocolate and is very bitter. If the cocoa butter is removed from the baking chocolate, powdered cocoa is produced.

Scientists have identified over 200 chemical compounds that contribute to the flavor of chocolate. Therefore, it is very difficult to make an artificial chocolate flavor. So most chocolate flavored items are made using cocoa powder or baking chocolate. The most common imitation chocolate flavor is made from carob, which is the fruit of a locust tree. However, most people will tell you that carob does not come close to the delicious flavor of the real thing. Similarly, scientists have developed an imitation vanilla that is produced from a sugar or wood fiber. It has the same chemical formula as the vanilla flavor, but has a bitter aftertaste that some people dislike.

Overall, most people, especially in Europe and America, are willing to pay for their favorite flavors of vanilla and chocolate. Are you hungry for a chocolate bar now?

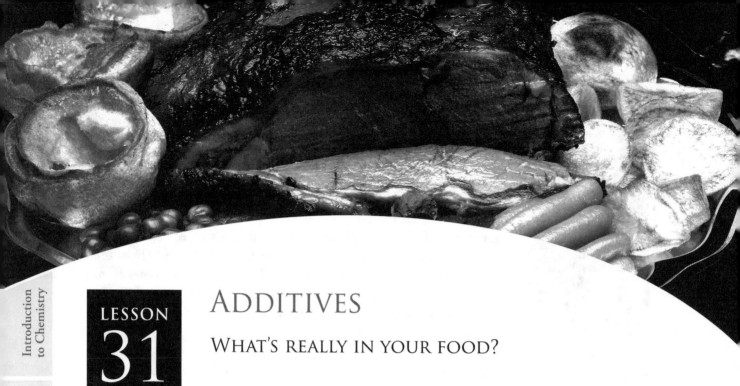

Introduction to Chemistry

Measurement of Matter

States of Matter

Classifications of Matter

Solutions

Food Chemistry

Unit Activity & Conclusion

LESSON

31

ADDITIVES

WHAT'S REALLY IN YOUR FOOD?

SUPPLY LIST:

Apple   Lemon juice

Unless you eat only fresh fruits and vegetables that are grown on organic farms, you probably have eaten chemical additives in your food. Chemicals are added to foods for many reasons. Some are added to keep the food from spoiling; others are added to improve the food's look, taste or texture.

For centuries people have added sugar or salt to their foods to keep them from spoiling. For example, sugar is added to fruit to make jams and jellies. Salt is added to meat to make jerky, bacon or ham. Sugar and salt work as preservatives because they absorb much of the moisture in the food. Bacteria need moisture to grow, so sugar and salt help to reduce bacteria growth.

Today, there are over 3000 different additives that are used in food products. These additives include preservatives, antioxidants, emulsifiers, stabilizers, flavorings and colorings. Vitamins and minerals are also added to many foods to improve their nutritional value.

Preservatives are added to keep food fresh and to prevent mold and bacteria from growing in the food. One common preservative is acid. Vinegar is added to cucumbers to make pickles. Vinegar is an acid that prevents bacteria from growing. In a similar way, antioxidants are chemicals that prevent food from reacting with oxygen. BHA and BHT are antioxidants that are often added to oils in very small amounts to prevent them from reacting with the oxygen and becoming spoiled.

Emulsifiers and stabilizers are chemicals that are added to change the texture of a food, usually to thicken it. Emulsifiers are often used to help prevent oil and water from separating. Natural emulsifiers include eggs, tree sap and seaweed. Artificial chemical emulsifiers include polysorbate and propylene glycol.

Flavors and flavor enhancers are added to improve the flavor of the food. You just learned about what flavors are and how chocolate and vanilla flavors are produced, but many other flavors are added to foods as well. Sugars or other sweeteners are often added to improve the flavor of a product. Hundreds of other natural and artificial flavors are used as well. Flavor enhancers are used to make the flavor stronger rather than to change it. A small amount of salt can enhance the flavor of a food. Another common flavor enhancer is MSG (monosodium glutamate), a compound originally made from seaweed, but today made from molasses.

Finally, colorings are added to many foods. Colorings do not have any nutritional value and do not change the flavor of the food, but can make the food more appealing. Many foods change color when they are heated. So frequently, colorings are added to processed foods to make them look more like we expect them to look. For example, strawberries turn brown when they are heated, so red food coloring is added to strawberry jam to make it more appealing. Certain shapes and colors suggest flavors and help us enjoy our food more.

The federal Food and Drug Administration (FDA) oversees the use of additives in food. Each manufacturer is required to perform tests to show that the additives they use are safe for humans. These findings are submitted to the FDA. Some additives are not added by the food manufacturer, however. Some chemicals get into the food when it is grown. This could include pesticides and herbicides as well as hormones given to animals. These items would not appear on a list of ingredients.

PRESERVING OUR FOOD:

Although many food additives do not add to the nutritional value of the food, some additives, such as preservatives, are very useful. To demonstrate the use of preservatives do the following.

Slice an apple into quarters. Spread lemon juice over all exposed surfaces on two of the pieces. Allow all of the pieces to sit exposed to the air for one hour. After one hour, compare the appearance of the pieces.

The lemon juice is an antioxidant, which means it prevents the molecules on the surface of the apple from reacting with the oxygen in the air. Therefore, the pieces covered with lemon juice remained white while the pieces without the lemon juice reacted with the oxygen to form molecules that turn brown. These molecules form a protective barrier that prevents the rest of the apple from spoiling, but gives the apple a brown appearance. Antioxidants in many foods keep the foods from spoiling.

The most nutritious food is always the fresh, unprocessed food that God created; however, it is not always possible to eat fresh foods, and preservatives keep foods from spoiling and allow us more convenience.

GOD'S DESIGN FOR CHEMISTRY
PROPERTIES OF MATTER

Introduction to Chemistry

Measurement of Matter

States of Matter

Classifications of Matter

Solutions

Food Chemistry

Unit Activity & Conclusion

GOD'S DESIGN FOR CHEMISTRY
PROPERTIES OF MATTER

Introduction to Chemistry

Measurement of Matter

States of Matter

Classifications of Matter

Solutions

Food Chemistry

Unit Activity & Conclusion

WHAT DID WE LEARN?

What is a food additive? (Anything that is added to the food by a manufacturer.)

Name three different kinds of additives. (Preservatives, antioxidants, emulsifiers, stabilizers, coloring, flavor enhancers, vitamins and minerals.)

Why are preservatives sometimes added to foods? (To keep the foods from spoiling.)

What compound has been used as a preservative for thousands of years? (Salt has been used to preserve many foods, especially meats. Sugar has also been used for a long time.)

Why are emulsifiers sometimes added to foods? (To keep the oil and water in the foods from separating. Remember when you made mayonnaise?)

TAKING IT FURTHER

Why are vitamins and minerals added to foods? (Processing, such as heating, often kills bacteria but also destroys many of the nutrients in the foods. Vitamins and minerals are often added back in to restore the nutritional value of the food.)

Why does homemade bread spoil faster than store bought bread? (Because it does not contain preservatives like the store bought bread does.)

Look at the labels on some food items in your kitchen. What are some of the common additives that you see? (The additives will vary considerably, but ingredients that end in "ose" are probably some sort of added sugar. If the list includes the word enriched, it means that vitamins and minerals have been added. Look for salt, sodium, MSG, BHT and BHA.)

FUN FACT

Americans eat an average of 150 pounds of food additives each year.

FUN FACT

50 percent of the products on grocery store shelves did not exist only ten years ago. This is primarily due to the extensive research into chemical additives. These additives are necessary ingredients in many products today. Of course this does not mean that many of the products are more nutritious, just that they are more convenient.

Introduction to Chemistry

Measurement of Matter

States of Matter

Classifications of Matter

Solutions

Food Chemistry

Unit Activity & Conclusion

BREAD

WHY IS IT LIGHT AND FLUFFY?

LESSON 32

SUPPLY LIST:

Flour
Yeast
Salt
Sugar
Spray oil

Butter or margarine
Water
Milk
Baking pan

If you mix some flour, water and yeast with a little sugar, butter and salt, you can make a loaf of bread. This delicious food is an important part of most diets around the world. The ancient Egyptians are credited with discovering that adding yeast to dough makes the bread rise and become fluffy. Today, fluffy bread is a staple in most American households.

Most bread in America is made from wheat flour. Wheat contains a protein called gluten. Gluten plays a very important part in the formation of bread. The other major ingredient in the bread we enjoy is yeast. Yeast is a type of fungi. Yeast reacts chemically with the sugar and starch in the bread dough and produces carbon dioxide gas. This reaction is called fermentation. The gluten in the flour allows the dough to stretch, and traps the carbon dioxide gas bubbles, thus allowing the dough to rise. When the bread dough is baked, the heat kills the yeast and the carbon dioxide escapes, leaving behind tiny air pockets that make the bread fluffy.

Bread contains many important chemical compounds. Mostly bread contains carbohydrates in the form of starch and a small amount of sugar. Bread also contains water, protein, fat, fiber, vitamins and minerals. In general, whole wheat bread is more nutritious than white bread because much of the wheat kernel is removed to make white flour.

Mixing the dough and allowing it to rise are important steps in the bread making process. But baking the dough is also very important. The

113

GOD'S DESIGN FOR CHEMISTRY
PROPERTIES OF MATTER

Introduction to Chemistry

Measurement of Matter

States of Matter

Classifications of Matter

Solutions

Food Chemistry

Unit Activity & Conclusion

type of starch found in flour is called beta-starch. Beta-starch is formed from long rigid chains of glucose that are bound tightly together. The beta-starch molecules have a crystalline structure that is hard to digest. So eating raw bread dough would not be a good idea. When the dough is baked, the heat causes the starch molecules to break down and water molecules get in between the starch molecules. These smaller molecules are called alpha-starch molecules.

Alpha starch gives the bread its pleasing smell and soft consistency. Also, the enzymes in your stomach more easily digest these smaller molecules. So baking is necessary to change bread dough into something wonderful to eat. As the bread gets old, the water evaporates from the bread and the alpha-starch molecules begin to revert back to beta-starch. This is why we don't enjoy eating stale bread. But if you enjoy a sandwich with nice soft bread, thank God for creating wheat with gluten and yeast to make the bread rise.

BAKING BREAD:

You can enjoy the wonderful chemical reactions that create bread by baking your own loaf of bread.

In a large bowl, combine 1 cup of flour, 2 tablespoons sugar, 1 package of active dry yeast (2 ¼ teaspoons) and 1 teaspoon salt. In a separate bowl or measuring cup, heat ¾ cup water, ¼ cup milk, and 1 tablespoon butter or margarine until very warm (120-130 °F). Gradually add the liquid to the dry ingredients, beating on low speed of an electric mixer until all the liquid is added. Then beat at high speed for 2 minutes, occasionally scraping the sides of the bowl.

With a spoon, stir in enough remaining flour to make a soft dough that is not sticky. Knead the dough on a lightly floured surface for 8-10 minutes until the dough is smooth and elastic, adding flour as necessary to form a smooth dough. Spray a large bowl with cooking oil. Place the dough in the bowl and turn the dough over so the top of the dough is greased. Cover. Let rise in a warm area until it doubles in size, about 30-60 minutes.

Next, form the dough into a loaf. On a floured surface, roll the dough into a 12 X 7 inch rectangle. Beginning at the short end, roll the dough tightly and place seam side down in a greased baking pan. Cover and allow to rise until double, about 1 hour. Put the loaf in the oven and bake at 400 °F for 30 minutes or until done. Remove from pan, allow to cool, then slice and enjoy!

WHAT DID WE LEARN?

If you want fluffy bread, what are the two most important ingredients? (Wheat flour that contains gluten, and yeast)

Why is gluten important for fluffy bread? (The gluten allows the bread dough to stretch and traps the gas produced by the yeast.)

Why does bread have to be baked before you eat it? (The baking process breaks down the long starch molecules into smaller molecules that are more easily digested.)

Why is whole wheat bread more nutritious than white bread? (The white flour does not contain all of the parts of the wheat kernel, so it has fewer nutrients.)

TAKING IT FURTHER

What would happen if you did not put any sugar in your bread dough? (The yeast would not be able to produce as much carbon dioxide gas, so your bread would not be as fluffy.)

Can bread be made without yeast? (Yes, other forms of leavening can be used such as baking soda or baking powder. However, the bread will be more like tortillas or pita bread than the fluffy bread you may be used to.)

GOD'S DESIGN FOR CHEMISTRY
PROPERTIES OF MATTER

Introduction to Chemistry

Measurement of Matter

States of Matter

Classifications of Matter

Solutions

Food Chemistry

Unit Activity & Conclusion

Bread Through the Centuries

Dinner rolls, crescent rolls, tortillas, sourdough, wheat, white, challah, pita and bagels are just a few of the many types of bread eaten around the world. Wheat flour is the most commonly used flour for making bread, but it is not the only flour used. Other flours are made from rye, buckwheat, barley, potato, rice, legumes, beans, quinoa, amaranth and nuts. In many cases, these other flours are mixed with wheat flour because of the high amount of gluten in wheat. But no matter the type of flour you use, you will be eating a food that has been around for thousands of years and has played an important part as a staple of life in nearly every culture.

Bread is not only important for food, it has become part of our vocabulary and is used in many common expressions. It is used symbolically in the Lord's Prayer, "Give us this day our daily bread," meaning our daily needs. We sometimes use the term *bread* to mean money when we refer to work as "our bread and butter." And you might hear someone say that something is the "bread of life," meaning it is very important for survival or happiness. All of this shows that bread is a vital part of survival and an integral part of our lives.

The process of baking yeast bread is thought to have started in Egypt and spread to the Greeks and Romans, then later to Europe. Bread was considered so important in Rome that it was put on a higher scale than meat. If soldiers were not given their allotment of bread they felt slighted or neglected. The Roman welfare system in the city of Rome was originally set up to hand out grain, but later the government started baking the bread before giving it to the people. Later, in the dark ages, white bread became popular. White bread was preferred by the noblemen and was more expensive than the darker whole wheat bread because of the added expense and work that went into making the flour white.

Bread has also played an important role in the Bible. In the book of Genesis, when

Melchizedek, a high priest of the Most High, came out to bless Abram, he brought with him bread and wine (Gen. 14:18). Later, when the Lord was passing by on his way to destroy Sodom, Abraham offered Him bread (Gen. 18:5). When Jacob made the meal for which Esau traded his birthright, it included bread and lentils (Gen. 25:34). On the night of the Passover, the Israelites were to eat meat with bitter herbs and unleavened bread. God said that each year at Passover His people were to celebrate by eating unleavened bread for seven days. This is called the Festival of Unleavened Bread (Ex. 12:8).

Bread is an important part of worship as well. When God gave instructions for the tabernacle He told them to put the Bread of the Presence on the table so it would be in front of Him all the time (Ex. 25:30). Unleavened bread made with olive oil was also a part of a grain offering to the Lord (Lev. 2).

Bread was also important in the life of Jesus. When Satan tried to tempt Jesus with bread, Jesus responded with, "Man shall not live by bread alone, but by every word that proceeds from the mouth of God" (Matt. 4:4). When Jesus was giving a sermon and the people got hungry, he took five loaves of bread and two fish and fed 5,000 men, plus the women and children with them (Matt. 14:16-21). But the most important reference to bread in the Bible is near the end of Jesus' life: "And as they were eating, Jesus took bread, blessed and broke it, and gave it to the disciples and said, 'Take, eat; this is My body.'" (Matt. 26:26) Jesus is the true bread of life.

FOOD CHEMISTRY QUIZ

LESSONS 28-32

Choose the best answer.

1. _____ Which is the most popular drink in the world?

   A. Tea   B. Water   C. Soda Pop   D. Coffee

2. _____ What is 70% of all soda pop sweetened with?

   A. Corn syrup   B. Saccharine   C. Sugar   D. Aspartame

3. _____ To guarantee that each can of soda tastes the same, what must a company do?

   A. Purify the water   B. Guard its recipe   C. Test the solutions   D. All of these

4. _____ Which of the following is not used to make soda pop?

   A. Corn Syrup   B. Flavorings   C. Carbon dioxide   D. Oxygen

5. _____ What accounts for the perceived flavor of a food?

   A. Chemical compounds   B. Color   C. Texture   D. All of these

6. _____ Which civilization is believed to be the first to enjoy chocolate?

   A. Egyptians   B. Aztecs   C. Romans   D. Greeks

7. _____ What is the purpose of fermenting vanilla beans?

   A. Keep harvesters busy   B. Change the color   C. Develop flavor   D. Kill bacteria

8. _____ Which of the following is a natural flavor?

   A. Bubble gum   B. Vanilla   C. Smoke   D. Spice

9. _____ How do additives help preserve food?

   A. Stop bacteria growth   B. Improve flavor   C. Change color   D. They don't

10. _____ Which of the following helps bread to be fluffy?

    A. Water   B. Butter   C. Yeast   D. Salt

11. _____ Which agency oversees the use of food additives?

    A. Dept. of Navy   B. FDA   C. IRS   D. Pentagon

12. _____ Which of the following makes bread easier to digest?

    A. Letting it age   B. Salt   C. Baking   D. Butter

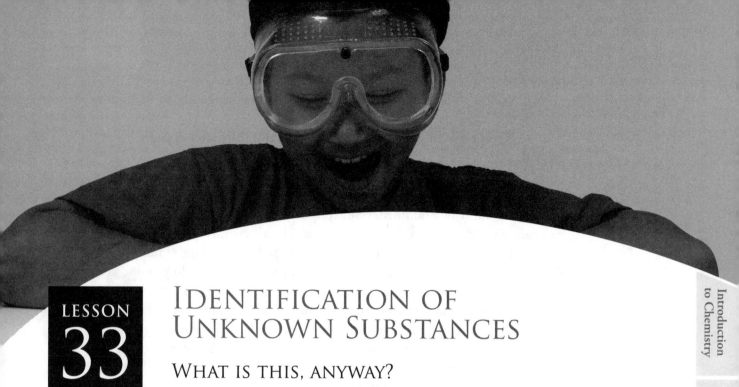

LESSON 33

IDENTIFICATION OF UNKNOWN SUBSTANCES

WHAT IS THIS, ANYWAY?

UNIT PROJECT SUPPLY LIST:

1 copy of "Identification of Solids" for each child (pg. 122)
1 copy of "Identification of Liquids" for each child (pg. 123)

Iodine	Vinegar
Baking soda	Water
Cornstarch	Rubbing alcohol
Powdered sugar	Vegetable oil

Now that you have learned many things about matter, you can begin to apply some of that knowledge. One way that you can use what you have learned about the properties of matter is to try to identify unknown substances. How does a scientist, even a young one, identify a substance without knowing what it is? You use the scientific method. First you learn about something, which is what you have been doing in the lessons in this book. Then you ask a question; in this case you want to know what the substance is. Third, you make a hypothesis. Based on what you know about how the substance looks you can make a guess as to what it is. Next, you design a way to test your hypothesis. Using what you have learned about matter, you can try different chemical tests to see how the substance reacts and to test if it is what you think it is. Finally, you see if your results support or contradict your hypothesis.

There are many different ways you can test a substance to see what it might be. First, you want to use your senses. Examine the substance's color, texture and viscosity. Carefully smell the substance. To do this, hold the substance about six inches from your nose and use your hand to push or wave some of the air from above the sample toward your nose. You do

119

GOD'S DESIGN FOR CHEMISTRY
PROPERTIES OF MATTER

Introduction to Chemistry

Measurement of Matter

States of Matter

Classifications of Matter

Solutions

Food Chemistry

Unit Activity & Conclusion

not want to take a big whiff because some substances can burn the inside of your nose.

Never taste an unknown substance! Many substances can be harmful.

These observations can be helpful; however, many substances look alike and may not have much of a smell. So other chemical and physical characteristics must be examined. Some physical and chemical tests can be very complicated and must be done by experienced scientists under controlled conditions. But others are relatively simple and can be done at home.

For example, you can measure the mass, density, boiling point and freezing point of many substances. You can also do some of the tests mentioned for chemical analysis of food, such as using iodine to test for starch or using brown paper to test for oils. You have also seen that vinegar reacts with baking soda to produce carbon dioxide bubbles. You can also test for acids and bases using the pigment from red cabbage as a reagent. These are all tests that you can do at home.

Some tests that scientists do that should not be done at home include flame tests and acid tests. Different substances give off different colors when a sample is placed in a flame. Also, certain metals react differently with various acids. Another way that scientists test unknown substances is with an instrument called a spectroscope. This instrument passes a beam of light through a prism and then the spectrum of light passes through the sample. The color or colors of light that pass through the sample are different for each substance, so this can be used to identify the substance.

Chemical analysis of substances is not only important for identifying unknown substances, but also for monitoring many manufacturing processes. Testing is done to ensure the quality of raw materials. This helps guarantee consistent results when manufacturing food and other items. End products are also tested to ensure quality and consistency. Chemical testing is used to test the purity of metals and dyes. It is used to test the amount of alcohol in liquor. And it is used to test the purity of our water supply. These are only a few ways that chemical analysis is used. Your food, clothing, appliances, building materials and nearly everything else around you has been tested by a chemical reaction before coming to you. All of this testing assures that the products you buy are safe and reliable. So be glad that God created matter to be consistent and to react the same way each time it is exposed to other chemicals.

UNIT PROJECT

IDENTIFYING UNKNOWN SUBSTANCES:

Set up the following two experiments. Complete each experiment using a copy of the "Identification of Solids" worksheet and a copy of the "Identification of Liquids" worksheet.

Experiment one: Number three plates or other containers with the

GOD'S DESIGN FOR CHEMISTRY
PROPERTIES OF MATTER

Introduction to Chemistry

Measurement of Matter

States of Matter

Classifications of Matter

Solutions

Food Chemistry

Unit Activity & Conclusion

numbers 1-3. On plate 1 place two tablespoons of cornstarch. On plate 2 place two tablespoons of powdered sugar. On plate 3 place two tablespoons of baking soda. (Do not tell your child which substance is which until after he/she has done the experiments on the worksheet. You may give younger children a list of substances from which to choose.)

Experiment two: Number three cups 1-3. Place ½ cup of water in cup 1. Place ½ cup of vinegar in cup 2. Place ½ cup of rubbing alcohol in cup 3. (Again, do not tell your child which substance is which until he/she has done the experiments on the worksheet. Again, you may want to give younger children a list of possible choices.)

Write a paragraph explaining what you learned from each experiment so you can share the results with others.

WHAT DID WE LEARN?

What method should be used in identifying unknown substances? (The scientific method)

Why should you avoid tasting unknown substances? (The substance can be dangerous or harmful, so you don't want to taste it if you don't know what it is.)

How can you test the scent of an unknown substance safely? (Hold it a few inches away from your nose and push some air toward your nose. This allows you to smell a few molecules without damaging your nose if the scent is very strong, like ammonia.)

What are some physical characteristics of an unknown substance you can test at home? (Mass, density, melting point, freezing point, boiling point and state—such as solid, liquid or gas)

What are some chemical characteristics you can test at home? (Presence of starch, oil, baking powder, acid or base)

TAKING IT FURTHER

Why is it important for food manufacturers to test the ingredients they use and final products they produce? (To ensure the safety and flavor of their foods)

Why is it important for water treatment facilities to test the quality of the water? (We don't want harmful bacteria or other dangerous substances in our water supply.)

IDENTIFICATION OF SOLIDS

Carefully observe each sample and write down your observations for each substance. Then add a few drops of water to a small sample of each substance. Feel each liquid and write your observations below.

Substance	Observations of dry sample	Observations of wet sample
1		
2		
3		

Now make a guess (hypothesis) about what you think each sample might be. It's okay if you find out that you are wrong—this is a learning experience. (Younger children can ask for a list of substances to choose from.)

Substance	What I think it is
1	
2	
3	

Think of some ways that you can test your hypothesis. Here are some suggestions: Test for starch using iodine. Test for baking soda by using vinegar. Test to see if each sample will dissolve in water. Be sure to use only a small amount of your sample for each test and write your results below.

Substance	Indicates starch?	Reacts with vinegar?	Dissolves in water?
1			
2			
3			

If you are still unsure about what each substance is, you can ask your teacher. Write the correct identification for each substance below.

Sample 1 is _____

Sample 2 is _____

Sample 3 is _____

Was your hypothesis correct? _____

IDENTIFICATION OF LIQUIDS

Carefully observe each sample and write down your observations for each substance. Be sure to include how the substance looks and smells.

Substance	How it looks	How it smells
1		
2		
3		

Now make a guess (hypothesis) about what you think each sample might be. It's okay if you find out that you are wrong—this is a learning experience. (Younger children can ask for a list of substances to choose from.)

Substance	What I think it is
1	
2	
3	

Think of some ways that you can test your hypothesis. Here are some suggestions. Test how fast it evaporates by dipping your finger in the liquid then letting it evaporate. If it evaporates quickly your finger will become cold. Test if it reacts to baking soda by dropping a few drops of each liquid on a sample of baking soda. Test its density compared to vegetable oil by adding a tablespoon of vegetable oil to each sample. If it is less dense than the oil the oil will sink. If it is denser than the oil, the oil will float.

Substance	Evaporates quickly?	Reacts with baking soda?	Denser than oil?
1			
2			
3			

If you are still unsure about what each substance is you can ask your teacher. Write the correct identification for each substance below.

Sample 1 is _____

Sample 2 is _____

Sample 3 is _____

Was your hypothesis correct? _____

PROPERTIES OF MATTER UNIT TEST

LESSONS 1-33

volume	mass	weight	solid
evaporation	gas	liquid	freezing
condensation	melting	viscosity	sublimation

Use the words above to help you fill in the blanks:

1. How much of a substance you have is its _____.

2. How much space something occupies is its _____.

3. How much gravity pulls on a mass is its _____.

4. The three states of matter are _____, _____ and _____.

5. When a liquid changes to a gas it is called _____.

6. When a solid changes to a liquid it is called _____.

7. When a liquid changes to a solid it is called _____.

8. When a gas changes to a liquid it is called _____.

9. When a solid changes directly to a gas it is called _____.

10. How thick a liquid is is called its _____.

Match the type of quantative measurement with the proper tool:

Volume of a liquid   meter stick

Mass   graduated cylinder

Weight   spring scale

Temperature   balance

Volume of a cube   thermometer

For each characteristic or statement, put E if it describes an element, C if it describes a compound or M if it describes a mixture. Some statements have more than one answer.

11. Cannot be broken into a smaller piece and still have its characteristics. _____

12. Contains two or more kinds of atoms. _____

13. Always has the same ratio of elements. _____

14. Iron _____

15. Water _____

16. Helium _____

17. Air _____

18. Seawater _____

19. Only 92 of these occur in nature. _____

20. Almost all substances on earth are these. _____

Identify each of the following changes as either a physical change (P) or a chemical change (C).

21. Burning of a candle _____

22. Rusting metal _____

23. Freezing of water _____

24. Crushing a graham cracker _____

25. Combining oxygen and hydrogen to make water _____

26. Rain falling from the clouds _____

Identify each characteristic as describing either a gas, a liquid or a solid. Some statements have more than one answer.

27. Molecules are far apart. _____

28. Has a definite shape. _____

29. Easily compressed. _____

30. Takes on the shape of its container. _____

31. Molecules are very close together. _____

32. Molecules slide over one another. _____

Short answer:

33. If a liquid is cooled will it be able to dissolve more or less solid? _____

34. If a glass of soda pop is very bubbly looking is it more likely to be warm or cold?

_____

35. What similar processes are required to produce the flavors of vanilla and chocolate?

_____

36. How can you tell if a solution is saturated? _____

37. How can you tell if a liquid mixture is a solution or a suspension? _____

_____

Introduction to Chemistry

Measurement of Matter

States of Matter

Classifications of Matter

Solutions

Food Chemistry

Unit Activity & Conclusion

CONCLUSION

A RELIABLE WORLD

LESSON 34

SUPPLY LIST:

2 balloons
Water
Candle

Think back about all the things you have learned about the matter that makes up this world and the universe. Matter was designed in such a way that particular substances always have the same physical and chemical characteristics. Pure water always boils and freezes at a particular temperature. Water is always made of one oxygen and two hydrogen atoms. Gold has a higher density than silver or bronze. Matter cannot be created or destroyed by any natural means.

All of these laws show that God is a loving creator. God created water to be the great solvent. He created our bodies to chemically react with the food we eat to provide energy. And God created the perfect recycling system when He made plants that use carbon dioxide and release oxygen and then made animals and humans that use oxygen and release carbon dioxide.

REFLECTING ON GOD'S WONDERFUL CREATION:

Let's do a final experiment to demonstrate God's love for us. One of the most important properties of water is its ability to hold heat. The temperature on earth is relatively stable and moderate compared to temperatures on other planets. This is due primarily to the fact the earth has an atmosphere and that over 70% of the surface of the earth is covered with water. Water gains and loses heat much more slowly than air does. This allows the temperatures along the coasts to be milder than inland areas, and allows the temperature on earth to be more moderate than on any other planet. To demonstrate this property of water, fill one balloon with air. Fill a second balloon with water. Tie each balloon closed. Carefully light a candle and hold the air-filled balloon over the flame. It quickly pops. Why? Because the air could not absorb the heat and the balloon quickly melted.

Now hold the water-filled balloon over the flame. Be sure the flame is under the part with water and not air. This balloon can absorb the heat for a long time. If you hold it long enough the water will even begin to boil. After 1-2 minutes remove the balloon and blow out the candle. Feel the balloon and you will see that it is slightly warm. The water was able to absorb the heat so quickly that the balloon did not melt or pop.

This demonstrates God's love and care. This property of water was not an accident. God designed it just for us to moderate the temperatures on earth. Take a few moments and reflect on the world and the matter it is made of, and thank God for His wonderful design.

WHAT DID WE LEARN?

What is the best thing you learned about matter?

TAKING IT FURTHER

What else would you like to know about matter? (Go to the library and learn about it.)

Introduction to Chemistry

Measurement of Matter

States of Matter

Classifications of Matter

Solutions

Food Chemistry

Unit Activity & Conclusion

Appendix A

Answers to Quizzes and Test

Introduction to Chemistry Quiz Answers:

Steps of the scientific method: A. 2 B. 1 C. 6 D. 4 E. 3 F. 5 Questions: 1. F 2. T
3. F 4. T 5. T 6. T 7. F 8. T 9. F 10. F Chemistry is the study of matter and how is reacts.

Measurement of Matter Quiz Answers:

1. mass 2. weight 3. conservation of mass 4. volume 5. density 6. buoyancy 7. balance 8.
spring scale 9. gold 10. water 11. Water is recycled. After a dinosaur drank water it exhaled
some water into the atmosphere. That water has been recycled through the water cycle for
thousands of years. 12. Nitrogen is absorbed by plants, eaten by animals, then returned to
the soil when the plant or animal dies. 13. The first liquid is denser than the second. 14. Use
the displacement method. 15. One substance is buoyant in another if it is less dense than the
other substance.

States of Matter Quiz Answers:

1. solid, liquid, gas 2. Adding heat 3. Removing heat 4. Removing heat 5. Adding heat 6. S, L
7. G 8. L, G 9. G 10. L 11. G 12. S 13. S, L 14. S 15. S, L 16. T 17. F
18. T 19. T 20. F 21. T 22. T

Classification of Matter Quiz Answers:

1. C 2. J 3. B 4. G 5. A 6. D 7. E 8. H 9. I 10. F 11. The fat molecules become unable to hold
the gas and it escapes. 12. Accept any reasonable answers. One likely answer is: Liquid water
does not act like oxygen gas or hydrogen gas. 13. Most substances will dissolve in water because
of its unique shape. 14. Carbon and hydrogen (1 carbon and 4 hydrogen atoms)

Solutions Quiz Answers:

1. T 2. F 3. F 4. T 5. F 6. T 7. T 8. F 9. T 10. T 11. Pressure pushes the molecules closer
together so the solute molecules will more easily combine and settle out of the solution. 12.
Pressure pushes the molecules closer together so the gas molecules cannot escape as easily. 13.
It is a dissolved substance that comes out of the saturated solution.

14. Salt lowers the freezing point of the ice, allowing it to absorb more heat from the ice
cream mixture and thus making the cream freeze more quickly. 15. The water will boil more
easily and could boil over if the temperatures get high. Also, water will freeze more easily and
could freeze in the winter time.

Food Chemistry Quiz Answers:

1. B 2. A 3. D 4. D 5. D 6. B 7. C 8. B 9. A 10. C 11. B 12. C

PROPERTIES OF MATTER UNIT TEST ANSWERS:

1. mass 2. volume 3. weight 4. solid, liquid, gas 5. evaporation 6. melting

7. freezing 8. condensation 9. sublimation 10. viscosity

Volume of a liquid – graduated cylinder, Mass – balance, Weight – spring scale, Temperature – thermometer, Volume of a cube – meter stick

11. E, C 12. C, M 13. E, C 14. E 15. C 16. E 17. M 18. M 19. E 20. M

21. C 22. C 23. P 24. P 25. C 26. P 27. gas 28. solid 29. gas 30. liquid, gas

31. solid, liquid 32. liquid 33. less 34. warm 35. Both require fermenting, aging and drying 36. No more solute will dissolve 37. If it is a suspension, particles will settle on the bottom; if it is a solution, there will be no settling.

Appendix B

Resource Guide

Suggested Library Books

Structure of Matter by Mark Galan in the *Understanding Science and Nature* series from Time-Life Books – Lots of real-life applications of Chemistry.

Inventions and Inventors series from Grolier Educational – Many interesting articles.

Soda Pop by Arlene Erlbach – Fun look inside a Soda Pop Factory.

Molecules by Janice VanCleave – Lots of fun activities.

Chemistry for Every Kid by Janice VanCleave – More fun activities.

Science Lab in a Supermarket by Bob Friedhoffer – Fun kitchen chemistry.

Science and the Bible, Volumes 1-3 by Donald B. DeYoung – Many experiments with great biblical applications of scientific ideas.

Exploring the World of Chemistry by John Hudson Tiner – An exciting and intriguing tour of chemistry with facts and stories about the discoveries and discoverers.

Suggested Videos

Newton's Workshop by Moody Institute – Excellent Christian science series, several titles to choose from.

Chemicals to Living Cell: Fantasy or Science (DVD) by Dr. Jonathan Sarfati – The laws of real chemistry show why "goo-to-you" evolution is impossible, available from *Answers in Genesis* (www.AnswersBookstore.com)

Science Supply Resources

R and D Educational Center
970-686-5744
www.rdeducation.com

Answers in Genesis
800-350-3232
www.AnswersInGenesis.org

Creation Science Resources

Creation: Facts of Life by Gary Parker – good explanation of the evidence for creation.

The Young Earth by John D. Morris Ph.D – evidence for a young earth.

The Answers Book by Ken Ham and others – answers the most common creation/evolution questions.

Field Trip Ideas

Visit a bakery

Visit a dairy farm to see where milk comes from

Visit a dairy bottling plant to see what happens to the milk after the farm

Visit a wastewater treatment plant

Visit a soda pop manufacturer

Visit a fresh-water treatment plant

Appendix C

Master Supply List

Supplies needed	Lesson	Supplies needed	Lesson
Baking soda	1,17, 24, 28, 33	Funnel	19
Vinegar	1, 22, 33	Liquid whipping cream	20
3 Empty soda bottles	2, 27	Vanilla extract	20, 24, 25
Yeast	2, 32	Can/spray whip cream	20
Molasses	2	Roll Lifesavers candy	21
Thermometer	2, 3	Rolling pin	21
Masking tape	2, 3, 5	Plastic zipper bags	21, 25, 27
Balloons	2, 15, 34	Dry mustard	22
Small box	3, 7	Paprika	22
Digital Stop watch	3	Lemon juice	22, 24, 31
2 Tennis balls	3, 14	2 Cans soda pop	23
Metric ruler, meter stick	3, 4, 5, 7	Food Coloring	24
Paper clips	4, 5	Club soda	24
Paper cups	5, 6	Corn Syrup	24
String	5	Nutmeg	24
Rubber band	5	Cinnamon	24
25 Pennies	5	Salt	25, 26, 32
Sugar cubes	6	Soda Straw	26
Ping-pong ball	8	Goggles	27
Golf ball	8	Sand	27
Rubbing alcohol	9, 33	Charcoal briquettes	27
Modeling clay	9	Cotton balls	27
Vegetable oil	9,13, 22, 29, 33	Alum	27
Popcorn	9	Hammer	27
Hand mirror	11	Apple	29, 31
Ice tray	11	Iodine	29, 33
Wooden block	12	Brown paper bag	29
Honey	12, 13	Bread	29
Hand lotion	13	Peanut butter	29
Dish soap	13	Potato or tortilla chips	29
Empty 1 gallon milk carton	15	Instant pudding mix	30
Jigsaw puzzle	16	Spray oil	32
2 small jars	17, 20	Powdered Sugar	33
Copper wire	17	Corn Starch	33
6-volt battery	17	Candle	34
Coffee filter	19		
Orange juice	19, 24		

It is assumed that other art supplies such as colored pencils, construction paper, markers, scissors, tape, etc. are available. Most other supplies should be readily available in most homes.

Appendix D

List of Reproducible Pages

Permission is granted to reproduce the pages listed below for single classroom use.

INDEX

Works Cited

Scientists: The Lives and Works of 150 Scientists. Ed. Peggy Saari and Stephen Allison. n.p.: U.X.L An Imprint of Gale, 1996.

Solids, Liquids, and Gases. Ed. Ontario Science Center. Toronto: Kids Can Press, 1998.

Ardley, Meil. *Making Metric Measurements*. New York: Franklin Watts, 1983.

Better Homes and Gardens New Cook Book. Des Moines: Merideth Corporation, 1981.

Biddle, Verne. *Chemistry Precision and Design*. Pensacola: A Beka Book Ministry, 1986.

Brice, Raphaelle. *From Oil to Plastic*. New York: Young Discovery Library, 1985.

Busenberg, Bonnie. *Vanilla, Chocolate, and Strawberry, The Story of Your Favorite Flavors*. Minneapolis: Lerner Publications Co., 1994.

Chisholm, Jane, and Mary Johnson. *Introduction to Chemistry*. London: Usborne Publishing, 1983.

Cobb, Vicki. *Chemically Active Experiments You Can Do at Home*. New York: J.B. Lippincott, 1985.

Cooper, Christopher. *Matter*. New York: Dorling Kindersley, 1992.

"Desalination of Water." *Columbia Encyclopedia*. 2000.

DeYoung, Donald B. *Science and the Bible*. Grand Rapids: Baker Books, 1994.

Dineen, Jacqueline. *Plastics*. Hillside: Enslow Publishers Inc., 1988.

Dunsheath, Percy. *Giants of Electricity*. New York: Thomas Y. Crowell Co., 1967.

Erlbach, Arlene. *Soda Pop*. Minneapolis: Lerner Publications Co., 1994.

"Farming , Food and Biotechnology." *Inventions and Inventors*. 2000.

Fleischmann's Yeast Best-Ever Breads. Birmingham: Time Inc. Ventures Custom Publishing, 1993.

"The Flour Page." *http://www.cookeryonline.com/Bread/flour.html*. June 2004: n.pag.

Friedhoffer, Bob. *Science Lab in a Supermarket*. New York: Franklin Watts, 1998.

Galan, Mark. *Structure of Matter - Understanding Science and Nature*. Alexandria: Time-Life Books, 1992.

"History." *http://www.breadinfo.com/*. June 2004: n.pag.

"How and Why Science in the Water." *World Book*. 1998.

Hughey, Pat. *Scavengers and Decomposers: The Cleanup Crew*. New York: Atheneum, 1984.

"International Vegetarian Union." *http://www.ivu.org/recipes/regions.html*. June 2004: n.pag.

Jenkins, John E., and George Mulfinger, Jr. *Basic Science for Christian Schools*. Greenville: Bob Jones University Press, 1983.

Julicher, Kathleen. *Experiences in Chemistry*. Baytown: Castle Heights Press, 1997.

Kuklin, Susan. *Fireworks: the Science, the Art, and the Magic*. New York: Hyperion Books for Children, 1996.

Mebane, Robert C., and Thomas R. Rybolt. *Air and Other Gases*. New York: Twenty-first Century Books, 1995.

"Medicine and Health." *Inventions and Inventors*. 2000.

Morris, John D., Ph.D. *The Young Earth*. Colorado Springs: Master Books, 1992.

Newmark, Ann. *Chemistry*. New York: Dorling Kindersley, 1993.

Nottridge, Rhoda. *Additives*. Minneapolis: Carolrhoda Books Inc., 1993.

Parker, Gary. *Creation Facts of Life*. Colorado Springs: Master Books, 1994.

Parker, Steve. *Look at Your Body - Digestion*. Brookfield: Copper Beech books, 1996.

Richards, Jon. *Chemicals and Reactions*. Brookfield: Copper Beech books, 2000.

Stancel, Colette, and Keith Graham. *Biology God's Living Creation Field and Laboratory Manual*. Pensacola: A Beka Books, 1998.

Steele, DeWitt. *Observing God's World*. Pensacola: A Beka Books Publishers, 1978.

Student Activities in Basic Science for Christian Schools. Greenville: Bob Jones University Press, 1994.

Thomas, Peggy. *Medicines from Nature*. New York: Twenty-First Century Books, 1997.

VanCleave, Janice. *Chemistry for Every Kid*. New York: John Wiley and Sons, Inc., 1989.

VanCleave, Janice. *Molecules*. New York: John Wiley and Sons, Inc., 1993.

Walpole, Brenda. *Water*. Ada, OK: Garrett Educational Corp., 1990.

"William Prout." *http://58.1911encyclopedia.org/P/PR/PROUT_WI*. 2004.

"William Prout." *www.thoemmes.com/encyclopedia/prout.htm*. 2004.

Ziegler, Sandra. *A Visit to the Bakery*. Chicago: Children's Press, 1987.